CENTRES FOR CURIOSITY AND IMAGINATION

John Pearce has been working in the field of community development and enterprise for over 30 years, both in the UK and overseas. Until 1991 he was chief executive of Strathclyde Community Business Ltd which was the major development and financing agency for community enterprises in the west of Scotland. He now runs his own consulting service, Community Enterprise Consultancy and Research. He has developed a community futures process to engage a cross-section of community stakeholders in the local development process and also a social auditing process tailored to the needs of small community and co-operative organisations.

John Pearce has written extensively about community development and enterprise and his book *At the heart of the community economy* was published in 1993 by the Calouste Gulbenkian Foundation. He is actively involved with the community enterprise movement in Scotland, serving as a director of Community Business Scotland and as chair of *New Sector* magazine. He is an active member of COMMACT, the Commonwealth Association for Local Action and Economic Development.

CENTRES FOR CURIOSITY AND IMAGINATION

When is a museum not a museum?

JOHN PEARCE

CALOUSTE GULBENKIAN FOUNDATION, LONDON

Published by the Calouste Gulbenkian Foundation
98 Portland Place
London W1N 4ET
Tel: 0171 636 5313

ISBN 0 903319 78 0

British Library Cataloguing-in-Publication Data
A catalogue record for this book is available from the British Library

Designed by Chris Hyde
Printed by Expression Printers Ltd, IP23 8HH
Distributed by Turnaround Publisher Services Ltd, Unit 3, Olympia Trading Estate, Coburg Road, Wood Green, London N22 6TZ. Tel: 0181 829 3000

ConTenTs

... break down inhibitions about the unknown ... an introduction to the broader world ... open to controversial issues and experimental adventures ... activate the intellectual and creative potential of children ... a catalyst for the process of learning ... geared to the emotional, physical and intellectual perspective of the child ... inspire learning through active play and exploration ... life-long love of learning ... experiment and experience at first hand the theories and principles taught in school classrooms start

Welcome
ਜੀ ਆਇਆਂ ਨੂੰ
स्वागत
স্বাগতম্
خوش آمدید
આવો પધારો
willkommen
bienvenue
croeso
fáilte
bienvenidos
benvenuti
witajcie
歡迎
ようこそ

Open:
Tuesday - Saturday 10 - 5
Sunday 2 - 5
Closed Mondays

Schools and Community
Groups welcome
Lift access through
Lending Library

Admission FREE

Walsall Museum and Art Gallery

photo: Gary Kirkham

The world of the child is shrinking and young children have less freedom of movement and therefore less freedom to explore. They are taken to school and back. They are accompanied to leisure pursuits, organised and supervised by adults. At home, television and the computer take over.

Children who are taught that the world is a dangerous place and who are denied opportunities, away from adults, for imaginative, unstructured play activities, for developing a sense of independence and confidence, and for negotiating their own relationships and arrangements, are unlikely to develop a positive sense of community or a capacity to contribute creatively to society. Yet today's children are the shapers of tomorrow.

These concerns led the Gulbenkian Foundation UK in 1990 to devote the main thrust of its social welfare programme to children: children's rights, children's welfare, children's education and development, and parenting. That policy commitment was based on the recognition that:

- children are 'individuals in their own right whose rights and interests simply cannot be subsumed within the broader needs of the family';

- 'too many young people are disillusioned with politics, alienated and marginalised from the process of power. Yet they are the future voters, and the future on which our society will depend';

- 'we need to equip our children with the necessary knowledge, skills and aptitudes ... to contribute as active players in a participative society.'[1]

In 1995 Paul Curno of the Foundation suggested that a research project might be undertaken in order to 'write a book describing the concept and operation of children's museums and exploring their potential for development in the United Kingdom by community enterprises, development trusts and local authorities'.

Children's museums are extensive and popular in the United States and the idea is taking hold in many other countries of the world. In Britain, however, they appear to be virtually unknown and apart from one very special example in Halifax (see Chapter three) they do not exist as such. Mention children's museums and few people know what you are talking of. Even those who have visited one in the United States are unlikely in the course of that visit to have comprehended the range of activities that is going on inside and outside the children's museum building. The very word 'museum' conjures up specific images in our minds which are far removed from the realities on the ground.

The research for this book has entailed making a number of field visits. During 1996 I visited Eureka! in Halifax and eight children's museums and two science museums in the United States. I also visited a number of museums, science centres and exploratories, visitor centres and related locations in Britain to explore contemporary presentations and exhibits in this country and compare them to the US children's museums. I attended the 1996 annual 'Interactivity' conference of the Association of Youth Museums, 'Building for the Future', in St Paul, Minnesota, as well as a special one-day pre-conference event for those considering how to start up a children's museum. In 1997 additional field visits were also made to seven children's museums in Berlin, Amsterdam and Rotterdam.

Many people have willingly given up time to meet and talk with me and to furnish me with many documents, reports and papers. I am most grateful to all of them and especially to all those who so generously shared their enthusiasm and ideas during our conversations at Interactivity 1996.

I travelled to the United States still unclear just what a children's museum was and rather sceptical about the phenomenon and its capacity for translation to the British context. In the event, I was both fascinated and impressed with what I saw and heard; and excited by the possibilities for replication. Within the growing movement in the United States there is an amazing diversity deriving largely from the 'localness' of each museum which will have evolved out of local circumstances, customs and needs. Notwithstanding this diversity there are key common characteristics which identify children's museums, an increasingly distinctive genre of institution. Whether 'museum' is the right word and whether these actually are museums is a debate which will run and run. Whatever its outcome, the fact is that they are popular and successful, and the principles and policies which underpin their approach and their work have obviously proved their worth.

I first visited the United States more than 15 years ago when, with some colleagues, I studied the community development corporations and other US approaches to community economic development. The 'travellers' tales' which we and many others brought back at that time have had a strong influence on what has since become a substantial social economy sector in the British economy encompassing various forms of community enterprise, community businesses and development trusts. I am confident that in the children's museums movement there are new ideas and possibilities, not to copy slavishly, but to adapt and mould to a British context.

•••••••••••••

The main intention of this report is to inform and, I hope, to stimulate an interest in the idea of children's museums in Britain.

Chapter one explores the definition of the phrase 'children's museum', identifies its key characteristics as evident in the United States experience and as expressed in a number of mission statements, and suggests that in Britain the term 'children's discovery centre' or 'children's discovery museum' may be preferred.

Chapter two describes the scale and nature of the children's museum movement in the United States and in particular the range of the exhibits, programmes and activities with which they become involved. It also looks at structure, finance, staffing, volunteering and community links and identifies some of the key issues facing the museums at this time.

Chapter three is about Eureka! and about the wider scene in Britain. Eureka! in Halifax is Britain's first and only acknowledged children's museum. The chapter outlines its history, describing the scale and nature of its present successful operation and identifying some of the key issues which arise from its origins and its current services. The chapter then surveys what is happening in Britain which is similar to the children's museum movement and notes that, while many specific services and facilities are available in this country, they are unlikely to be provided in an integrated fashion as they are in the United States with its community-based children's museums.

Chapter four takes a glance into Europe and beyond, at the growing world-wide interest in children's museums, and identifies some of the key contrasts and differences between European and US practice.

Chapter five identifies and enlarges on the key characteristics which a 'true' children's museum might be expected to incorporate. It considers the differing contexts in the United States, the United Kingdom and Europe concluding that there is an opportunity for us to learn from the US experience and to act upon it. It also emphasises that although children's museums may be called 'museums' they are quite different from 'traditional' museums, performing a different role and in no way competing with them. A number of measures are proposed which will first, promote a greater understanding and knowledge of the concept of the children's museum; second, opportunities for creating British models; and third, offer practical support for the establishment of children's museums in this country.

•••••••••••••

I am truly grateful to the Gulbenkian Foundation for the opportunity to discover the world of children's museums. I received a most warm welcome in the United States and in the European countries I visited and I was struck by the enthusiasm for their projects of everyone I met. There is something infectious in that enthusiasm and I hope that this book will serve not only to inform, but also to infect others with a determination to find out more and to consider creating their own local children's museum in towns and cities throughout Britain.

I must thank Paul Curno for his guidance, understanding and help during this project and also my son, Matthew, who accompanied me on the United States tour of museums and carried out some of the field interviews and visits in Britain, including taking two parties of children to Eureka! The Thorold family did some field research for me in New England and Henry and Lydia reported comprehensively on their visit to Eureka! Kay Caldwell, David Collett, Paul Curno, Joanna Pearce, and Harry Shier all read the first draft and I am grateful for their valuable comments. Denny Robson has guided the shaping of the research material into its present form and has been a source of continuous advice and help. The interpretations and conclusions remain, however, my own.

John Pearce
Harburn
March 1998

INSIDE THINGS

photo: Eureka! The Museum for Children

'Museum: a building dedicated to the pursuit of learning or the arts; a building used for storing and exhibiting objects illustrative of antiquities, natural history, art, etc.' *Shorter Oxford English Dictionary*

There is a problem with using the word 'museum' in relation to children's museums. For most people it is the second part of the definition above that comes to mind: 'a building used for storing and exhibiting objects ... etc' and that shapes our perception of what a museum is. Children's museums, however, have developed into a new genre of institution providing a range of facilities and services, primarily targeted at children. In doing this they have stretched to the limit – and perhaps beyond – the meaning and usefulness of the word 'museum'.

In the United States and Europe the term 'children's museum' has come to be the one most commonly used for the very special type of institution which is described and explored in the following pages. The panel below shows, however, that for many people 'children's museum' is not the right phrase – but there is no agreement about what is or might be 'right'. The most common other name is 'children's discovery centre' or 'children's discovery museum'. However for some that implies a science focus and one of the characteristics of a US-style children's museum is, as we shall see, the way it combines many facets.

The Children's Discovery Museum	The Curious Kids Museum
Kidspace Museum	Discovery House
Discovery Factory	Explorer Children's Museum
Kidcity	Children's Curiosity Museum
Discovery Centre	The Imaginarium
Imagination Station	Eureka!
The Discovery Place	Curioxity
Wonder Workshop	The Exploratory
Wonderscope	

In the following pages the term 'children's museum' is employed because that is what most, though not all, of the institutions studied in the United States and in Europe call themselves. In Britain, it may well be that the term children's discovery centre or children's discovery museum will become the accepted generic term in the future.

It is generally accepted that the modern history of children's museums began in 1962 when Michael Spock went to the Boston Children's Museum as Director and introduced new thinking and new ideas based on the principle that children and young people should learn for themselves through exploration and experience, through exhibitions that encouraged touching, feeling, smelling and doing as well as seeing. His 'landmark' interactive exhibit, 'What's Inside?' set the pattern not only for future exhibits at Boston but also throughout the museum world. The Children's Museum of Boston now claims to be 'the pioneer in the use of interactive exhibits that replaced glass cases with objects that people can touch and experience, a format adopted by museums everywhere today'.[1]

The basis of all children's museums is interactivity: learning by doing, learning through fun, learning through play. That hands-on approach has indeed spread throughout the traditional museum and art gallery world (although not as extensively and as uniformly as might have been expected). It has also spread into the commercial world of visitor centres, theme parks, tourist experiences and 'pay for play' organisations. In particular science museums and 'exploratories' have embraced interactivity to demonstrate how things are and how things work. 'Please touch', or at least 'Please press the buttons', has replaced 'Please do not touch' in many situations.

But children's museums are about much more than being a fun place based on interactivity. Interactivity is the *means* to stimulate and facilitate learning, especially for the under-12s: learning about society, about life, about past, present and future, about everything and anything that the particular children's museum considers relevant and important. The learning mission is central to all children's museums, and related to that is the mission to act as an educational resource in the local community. Equally, children's museums have a strong commitment to offer support to parents and to families.

Children's museums also play an important role in the social fabric of their community, as a venue for birthday parties, for entertainments or for cultural events. They involve hundreds of volunteers as well as employing staff. They run activities for teenagers, and outreach programmes in low income and remote neighbourhoods. They seek to ensure that no one is barred from attending or participating for lack of the entrance fee.

Children's museums come in a range of sizes from a few hundred square feet of exhibition space to over 100,000. Some operate 'without walls', putting all their effort into taking exhibits to different venues in their locality and concentrating on outreach

photo: John Pearce

Opened in 1913, the Children's Museum of Boston is the second oldest children's museum in the United States.

work rather than on acquiring permanent premises. Some are entirely run by volunteers or by only a handful of staff. Others have professional staff organised into specialist departments. Some are wholly financially self-sustaining, others remain substantially dependent on fund-raising and grants from the public sector.

In Chapter two we shall describe in detail the activities and programmes of the museums in the United States and the ways in which they are established and operate. Notwithstanding their diversity all are local institutions with strong community roots. They focus on children in a way that does not divide them from society, but enables adults and children to play, work and learn together.

The debate about education and collecting is an old one in the museum world. In *Cabinets of Curiosity*, Sara Selwood calls it the 'perennial conflict between elitism and populism'. She continues:

> 'The proponents of populism, concerned to provide the greatest access to the arts to the maximum number of people, identify education as the most important function of the museum ... The opposite view is that museums are fundamentally concerned with collection, preservation and scholarly research.'[2]

Certain children's museums emphasise that they *are* museums and therefore stress the importance of having collections. Indeed, they see having a collection and a curatorial policy as the hallmark of a 'real' museum. Others emphasise the social purpose of the institution and its role as a *community project*, responding to needs and opportunities in the community to benefit children and young people.

Jane Jerry (Children's Museum of Houston) writing in *Hand to Hand*, the journal of the Association of Youth Museums, argues for the importance of collections and for the name 'museum':

> 'To call ourselves museums is to give credence to the fact that we use objects to create exhibits in order to help children to learn – the objects in those exhibits need care. As museums, we are part of a unique educational profession, set off from schools, libraries and recreational centers. As museums, we have a responsibility to the objects we own and to the objects we borrow. Therefore it follows that although some of us do not own permanent collections, we still need to be cognizant of commonly accepted museum practices that pertain to collections management and we need to develop collection policies and collection management procedures that address our unique collections.'[3]

Ann Lewin (Capital Children's Museum, Washington), writing in the same issue, argues with a different emphasis that 'the key role of objects is to serve children's developmental needs, not to serve as artefacts for collections, preservation and exhibition'. She goes on to suggest that the name 'museum' is not important provided that the role of the children's museum is accorded the seriousness it deserves:

> 'I do not care if, in the minds of some, this attitude towards collecting makes us "not a museum". However, I protest if this attitude is interpreted as children's museums being merely "playspaces", especially if that word is used to put down the importance of a "children's museum" vis-a-vis a "real" museum. I protest because playspaces can be the most powerful environments to enhance learning in people of any age and to stimulate rich adult/child interaction. Pejoratively labelling museums which do not collect as "playspaces" misses the meaning of what a playspace is.'[4]

A further dimension to this definitional debate is the concept of the children's museum operating as a community centre:

> 'What comes to mind when you hear "children's museum"? Is it job training and career counselling? How about community service and social activism? Or maybe peer mentoring and multicultural education? Children's museums, known for their child-centred exhibits and programs, are evolving to become community centers for the 1990s, providing services for children and families, once the mission of local, state and federal agencies. As budget cuts in education and the social services mean less for children and families, institutions like children's museums are rising to meet the challenge.'[5]

The debate will run and run, probably without resolution. Children's museums are not museums in the traditional sense. They are different in their missions, in their approach and in their specifically targeted age-group. While they share features with traditional museums (for example they exhibit and educate) and some certainly also collect and store, they also have a community and social role. They are very diverse, reflecting different emphases and different local circumstances. They change over time. The slogan on the banner in front of the Children's Museum Boston says: 'Kids keep changing. So do we.'

Four key characteristics may be defined which act as a common thread for all children's museums, which encapsulate their distinctiveness and which, despite the diversities, link them as one genre of institution.

- First, they focused on serving the needs of children, for the most part up to 12 years old, although a small minority do run programmes for teenagers.

- Second, although they are child-focused, they are equally institutions for the family offering opportunities for children and adults together.

- Third, they aim to encourage learning – through discovery, through play, through fun, through hands-on exploration, through interaction with things and with people.

- Fourth, they are rooted in their local communities, reflecting local circumstances, cultural and ethnic traditions and needs.

We now turn to look at what this means in practice in the United States.

photo: John Pearce

Imagination is more important than knowledge. *Albert Einstein*[1]

One day when Pooh Bear had nothing to do, he thought he would do something ... [2]

The children's museums movement has grown significantly in recent years in the United States. The Association of Youth Museums (AYM – see Appendix one) estimates that there are some 200 children's museums operating in the United States and more are opening all the time.

The largest children's museum in the United States is the Children's Museum of Indianapolis with an exhibition space of 122,825 square feet within a building of 325,000 square feet. It has 180 full-time and 200 part-time staff who are supported by 1,575 volunteers. Annual attendance is over 900,000 visitors and the annual operating budget is $11,400,000.

By contrast, the Chesapeake Museum in Maryland simply has a rent-free unit in a shopping mall, receives 11,000 visitors annually, operates with a budget of $40,000 and has one paid post shared by five people each working on one day per week, while

A variety of exhibits

kidtown ... make it, take it ... treehouse ... spirit of Native American ... body works ... just for tots ... discover your world ... $H_2OH!$ ... reaching for the stars ... bubbles ... Utah centennial map ... African impressions ... a journey through time ... lunar lander ... bubble-izer ... the cave ... passage of time ... tree and me ... fire pole and bell ... Kissimnee valley man ... the good knight castle of Avalon ... wet 'n' wild ... luckey's climber ... cows, curds and their wheys ... life in a creek ... inventions by Leonardo da Vinci ... stick out your tongue ... communication station ... bugs R us ... street where you live ... momentum machine ... great grandmother's kitchen ... kid's farm ... inventors' workshop ... body basics – the inside story ... space shuttle ... cog city ... step into the past ... habitot ... kid-tv ... rainbow room ... 1890s store ... up with puppets ... Stuffee ... Ms Frizzle's magic school bus ... dress-up shop ... science tower ... little yellow house ... farmer's market ... harmonograph ... the river that flows both ways ... slice of the city ... the walking piano ... soundsations ... the world of Pooh ... ranch house under construction ... grocery store and skyscraper the Children's Museum of Acadiana operated 'without walls' from 1990 until it eventually moved into its first premises ('behind Don's Seafood-Downtown') in January 1996.

The target age range for children's museums is primarily the under-12s with an emphasis on the four to eights. A majority of children's museums are located in urban or suburban areas, with few claiming a rural location. It is not unusual for a children's museum to be located in a shopping mall and a significant number have developed their premises within a downtown revitalisation programme.

Exhibits: content and design

Children's museums have developed a wide range of different exhibits over the years. The range of the titles which are used to describe exhibits (see panel on page 23) shows both the variety of the exhibits and the inventiveness in naming them.

It is not surprising that there are common exhibit themes and contents. At the 1996 AYM Start-up pre-conference day the 10 most popular themes were listed as:[3]

1   Stores: grocery, general
2   Bubbles
3   Hospitals/clinics
4   Waterworks
5   Grandmother's attic/kitchen
6   Science labs
7   Recycling exhibits
8   Construction exhibits
9   Creativity centres
10 Theatre/studios

Although there will always be a search for new ideas and new themes, and for different ways of treating old themes, there is plenty for the start-up group to learn simply by visiting existing museums.

Quality and design will vary according to the resources available to the museum. Those which have only just started are likely to have made their own exhibits and a great deal of DIY 'sweat equity' will be contributed in this way by founder members of the museum. As museums become better established some will retain this principle of designing, developing and constructing their own exhibits and will have a permanent in-house exhibit team.

photo: Ulster Museum

'Stuffee', a creation from Pittsburgh Children's Museum, is a huge fabric doll which unzips to reveal a complete set of internal organs. Stuffee has been sold worldwide, including to the Ulster Museum's Science Discovery Bus (see page 73).

The Children's Museum, Boston: case study

CMB opened its doors in 1913, set up by the Boston Science Teachers Bureau, a group of teachers who believed that learning need not be confined to the classroom. The CMB is the second oldest children's museum in the United States and its original basis was a natural history collection, starting with one display case of birds and another holding minerals and shells.

In 1962 Michael Spock was appointed as the museum director and initiated an interactive exhibit philosophy based on the idea that direct access to real objects and materials enhances learning. This was the start of the 'hands-on' revolution in museum practice which has given Boston its reputation as a pioneer of participatory programmes and exhibits.

In 1979 the museum moved into a nineteenth-century brick and timber former warehouse in the heart of Boston's downtown waterfront area, well served by public transport. Here the museum has 35,000 square feet of exhibition space where its primary target age range is now children of two to 11 years, although in the past it has also targeted older children and young people.

Exhibits in spring 1996 included: boats afloat!; build it; a two-storey climbing structure; community gallery; dress-up shop; El Mercado Del Bario; giant's desk top; grandparents' house; hall of toys; Japanese house; kids' bridge (about the city's cultural and ethnic diversity); playspace (for younger children); science playground; teen Tokyo; TV and me; under the dock (underwater seascape); weaving and We're still here (about Native American history and culture, past and present). Some Boston-designed exhibits have been made available for hire or franchise to other children's museums throughout the United States.

Within the museum there is also a KidStage for real and play performances; a teachers' resource centre and a parents' resource centre. Every Friday is 'sleep-over' night and the buildings can also be rented for private functions.

CMB runs an extensive educational and outreach programme. These include: interdisciplinary teaching kits on more than 100 topics for hire to schools; teachers' training workshops; a child development programme; a science studies project; taking museum exhibits and activities to children's hospitals, day centres and low-income neighbourhoods; involvement in neighbourhood festivals. More than 3,000 group visits are booked annually from schools, pre-school groups and special needs groups. The May 1996 programme highlights, in a full calendar, included: Japanese tea ceremony and demonstration; the Big Apple circus; various KidStage presentations (Take me along; What's in a name? Why rat comes first; The three little pigs) and Kids are Cooking!

The museum places a special emphasis on recognising and serving the multicultural community of Boston. Its Multicultural Initiative aims 'to make the museum increasingly useful to and reflective of a diverse audience'. Similarly the Native American Programme emphasises a commitment to the Native American people of New England.

CMB holds a Cultural collection (30,000 objects) representing the daily lives of people and cultures around the world, and a Natural History collection (10,000 specimens). Its 'Study Storage' method of open storage permits visitors to examines items closely without danger of damage to the articles.

The museum receives 400,000 visitors each year while its programmes and services are used by a further 250,000 customers. Through its reduced admissions policy (including special group subsidies and free entrance in certain circumstances) the museum seeks to ensure that it is accessible to the widest audience possible.

The 1996 operating budget was $4.5m of which 60% is earned from admissions, memberships, sales and contracts. The remaining 40% is fund-raised or covered by endowment income or by grant aid from the state or federal funds or from foundations. There is a large and well-stocked shop but no café. However McDonalds are next door (by design) and a fast-food booth operates on the waterfront piazza of the museum.

There are 125 staff of whom 75 are part-time. Staff are organised into six departments: Programme and Evaluation; Education; Visitor Services; Public Relations and Marketing; Human Resources; and Development.

The CMB is an independent, non-profit tax exempt organisation with a board of 35 trustees, of whom eight serve on an executive committee. There is also a board of overseers, effectively an advisory body, of some 70 people.

The Children's Museum of Maine is particularly proud of its 'made in Maine' tradition. Everything in its new museum was designed and built by local people, museum staff and local firms, although the content and style of the exhibits are similar to those found in museums elsewhere. The Children's Museum of Minnesota, which has recently relocated in downtown St Paul into a brand new purpose-built building giving 20,000 square feet of exhibition space, has been entirely designed and fitted out internally by the museum's own exhibits development team.

Museums can take advantage of the development work done by other museums and buy or rent complete exhibits. Sometimes these will be replicas, and sometimes they will be an original which has moved on. Boston's acclaimed 'Kids' Bridge' which deals with cultural and ethnic diversity and recently closed in Boston is on tour via the Smithsonian Travelling Exhibition Service based in Washington DC. At Interactivity '96 the Staten Island Children's Museum was advertising three travelling exhibits for rent: 'It's news to me', 'Wonder water', and 'Tales in tall trees', while the Pittsburgh Children's Museum was advertising 'The Andy Warhol myths series and studio' and 'Building bridges: the art of Jerry Pinkney'. 'Stuffee', another creation from Pittsburgh, is a seven foot fabric doll which unzips down the front to reveal a complete set of internal organs. Stuffee has been sold world-wide, including to the Ulster Museum's science discovery bus.

Museums emphasise the vital importance of regular and efficient maintenance. In a 'hands-on' museum it is essential that things work. For this reason museums tend to eschew hi-tech exhibits, leaving those to the science museums, and prefer simpler, hardwearing items. Nonetheless, maintenance will be a substantial line in the annual budget.

Exhibits need to be renewed and replaced on a regular, programmed basis, which is also costly. The Discovery Museums at Acton, Massachusetts aim to renew/change one exhibit room (gallery) each year. The Children's Museum of Boston aims to change between four and six exhibits each year and in fact between September 1994 and December 1995 changed over 50%. Museums report that it is the children who are least enthusiastic about change – they like to be able to come to see the same, well known things. It is their parents who want to see something different, perhaps to demonstrate that they are getting their money's worth!

In addition to exhibits designed for the target age-group, museums recognise the need to provide some form of dedicated toddler space, especially as many parents of infant school age children also have younger toddlers.

Acton Discovery Museums' exhibit specification

1 Interactive The user must perform some kind of action to engage with the exhibit to which the exhibit will respond. Different kinds of actions elicit different responses from the exhibit.

2 Open-ended Ideally, there will be an infinite number of ways to use the exhibit. This way an individual – a very young child at CDM, or a youth or a PhD physicist at SDM – will find ways to engage the exhibit on their own levels. It also allows for an aspect of 'come-back-ability'. When an exhibit can be approached on many levels in limitless ways, visitors can use the exhibit on return visits in new ways. Exhibits promote feelings of success and wonderment for very young children, and promote interaction between parent and child and co-operation between children.

3 Multisensory Exhibits ideally appeal to many senses so that people with different learning styles find that they can engage with them in satisfying ways. Small children tend to be dominated by tactile and kinaesthetic impressions, hearing- or sight-impaired visitors may also approach exhibits through these senses as well as through visual and auditory impressions.

4 Self explanatory, self directed It should be evident how to begin to interact with the exhibit. There is no right or wrong way to approach an exhibit, and children should feel safe to explore. This can be accomplished through the design of the exhibit itself, the use of everyday objects that people know how to use, and through exhibit graphics (though not necessarily text because people rarely read signs in museums). Children often find ways to use exhibits that adults and designers never thought of.

5 Harmonise with nearby exhibits and themes The exhibit should reinforce concepts and phenomena illustrated by others in that particular theme area, creating a more in-depth experience. This way, an abstract concept like 'sound is vibration' can be reinforced by several exhibits that allow you to see, feel and hear how different vibrating objects cause sound and how sounds cause objects to vibrate. Theme rooms at CDM set boundaries for children which empower them to explore more confidently.

6 Developmentally appropriate Theme rooms at CDM include activities to use gross and fine motor skills. Both of these skills are important for pre-school age exploration and development.

7 Familiar Children's exhibits use familiar materials that promote accessibility and safety. Theme rooms must be warm and inviting. Science exhibits should look like something you could make at home with hardware store parts. The components and moving parts should be visible so there are no 'black boxes'. This serves to demystify science by using household items wherever possible so that science is thought of as part of everyday life rather than something only encountered in schools and laboratories.

8 Clean and working Exhibits should be designed and built with adequate access and appropriate design to be easily maintained and cleaned. If not, then they will be often broken and dirty.

9 Safe At CDM a choke tube test is used to eliminate small components. How children explore is considered in determining safety criteria. There should be no unexpected sharp edges, no splinters, no chance of electric shocks, falling, etc. Where potential hazards exist, supervision and protective gear will be provided.

10 Accessible – handicapped and culturally Exhibits should be able to be engaged as much as possible from wheelchairs, by people who are deaf, blind, retarded, autistic, or are non-English speakers. Signage is in English, though reading is not required to use the exhibits.

11 Inexpensive In-house generated exhibits are generally less expensive, and are more successful. Staff designs tend to break less often, require less and easier maintenance, along with offering more visitor interaction.

Exhibits must be designed with different skills and abilities in mind. The Discovery Museums at Acton tackle this issue partly by having two different buildings: the Children's Discovery Museum (CDM) aimed at toddlers and pre-schoolers and the Science Discovery Museum aimed at the six to 12s. Even so, Acton emphasises the need for exhibits to be 'open-ended' – that is, capable of interpretation and being understood in different ways by people of different ages, educational attainment and intellectual levels. It must also allow for and even encourage what Acton's director calls the 'ah-ha' experience: when the child (or adult) realises much later, after the museum visit, the why or the how of a particular activity. The Acton Discovery Museums have a very detailed exhibit specification (see panel on page 29) which is designed to ensure that the exhibits in the two museums relate to their educational mission.[4]

The huge floor map of Rhode Island to be found in that museum's 'State Room' is for young children a wonderful network of roads and rails on which to push cars, trucks and trains. But for older children (and parents) it is an accurate map from which to observe the cartographic details of the State.

At the 1996 AYM Start-up pre-conference a list of nine check answers[5] was offered to the question 'why do we do certain exhibits?' Because ...

1 They fit our museum's mission.
2 They embody the learning theories.
3 They incorporate the museum's educational philosophy/methodology.
4 They are relevant to our community.
5 They are age-appropriate and meet the needs of our children.
6 They are popular with children.
7 They can be done within existing resources.
8 They are maintainable and/or easy to repair.
9 They are interactive.

Looking as well as touching

The issue of whether to collect or not was explored in Chapter one. The reality is that some museums do and others do not, and that some acquire a collection by chance, through gift or bequest. The major practical constraint for any children's museum considering the collection question is whether it has adequate storage space and staff or volunteer resources available to care for a collection. The key question, however, is *how collections might be used.* The Children's Museum of Boston has devised a method of storage which substantially reduces the secrecy of 'behind closed doors'. Objects which require to be stored with care and which are not available for unrestrained use are kept in glass-walled areas so that museum visitors can see them and/or the storage system, and can see researchers and others having access to them for purposes of their work.

Boston, and other museums, also include exhibits which are to be looked at rather than touched. 'Looking, and not touching, can be fun' is how the Boston Museum Profile comments on its 'Hall of Toys' which features its extensive collection of dolls:

'A myriad of details are tucked into every scene waiting to be discovered.' The Children's Museum of Easton displays its current theme exhibit ('different cultures around the world' in May 1996) throughout its former fire station building. The exhibit consists primarily of models, drawings, collages and borrowed objects to be observed. The Children's Museum of Portsmouth (New Hampshire) likewise has a changing exhibit of art or craft, combining material to be observed with its other exhibits, which are very hands-on.

Combining looking with interactivity is a means of introducing children to the realities of other museums and galleries, where for the most part objects are to be observed and information is absorbed by looking and by reading.

Local community themes

In addition to the 'standard' themes, most museums develop exhibits which are especially relevant to their local community or which reflect contemporary issues. The Children's Museum of Boston has worked hard to recognise and respond to the multicultural reality of the Bostonian population: 'Because many children growing up in the greater Boston area today live in a diverse world, we have been working for many years to make their experience in the museum a multicultural one ... By the word multicultural, I mean a place where all people are valued and welcomed, where multiple perspectives are encouraged, and where board, staff audience and program reflect the community in which we live'.[6] The Kids' Bridge exhibit was designed to teach children to 'value their own race and ethnicity, as well as others', and to work against discrimination'.[7] 'TV and me' 'explores the impact and issues of television today. Children and parents learn how to take control of what they watch on television.'[8]

Following a local outburst of racial violence in 1991, which was sparked by a fatal motor car accident and was followed by a retaliatory attack, the Brooklyn Children's Museum became involved, with other organisations, in a project entitled 'Bridging Eastern Park Way: the Crown Heights History project', the title referring to the major street which symbolically divides the community. The project sought to present 'the contemporary history and experience of living in this diverse urban community through the eyes of local residents.'[9] The museum came to the conclusion that the project was not about race relations but 'about how people create and maintain their identities while co-existing in a shared space. And about how sharing this space can lead to misunderstanding and sometimes conflict'.[10]

The emphasis on 'localness' is reflected in many ways. 'Under the dock' with its giant lobsters and other sea creatures is about the underwater eco-system in the Boston harbour. The Rhode Island 'State Room' is both a geography and a local history exhibit. Local history is the theme of a horse and carriage ride offered by the Children's Museum of Portsmouth in association with a local livery company and there is a walk back to the museum following a route of historical associations.

In many museums there is an environmental and/or recycling exhibit. Boston's recycle project shop has 50 barrels of raw materials discarded by industry which are sold in bulk at low rates for reuse in schools, in playgroups, in families – anywhere where children and adults want to experiment with craft, design and creation.

The Children's Museum of Houston: mission statement

The purpose of the Children's Museum of Houston is to ignite a lifelong passion for learning through educational exhibits that provoke curiosity and inspiration.

Through multilingual and non-verbal information, the museum encourages hands-on experimentation by listening, touching, tasting, smelling and role-playing, as well as looking. Personal interaction among children and adults of varying ages, backgrounds and abilities enables museum visitors to gain self-esteem. The museum encourages the inventor in every child and strives to delight the child in every visitor.

The Children's Museum is a private, non-profit educational institution where children and families learn about history and culture, health and human environment, science and technology, and the arts. It is also a resource centre for parents, for childcare workers and educators. It provides materials about parenting and education, and collaborates with other community organisations to teach the role of museums.

The Children's Museum of Houston acknowledges its responsibility to the burgeoning field of new participatory children's museums and will provide support to that field according to the museum's resources. The Children's Museum strives to encourage and maintain a high level of quality among new children's museums according to commonly accepted museum practices.

Layout and access

The layout of any museum is of course determined by its building, and there are many examples of imaginative use of space. The Acton Children's Discovery Museum has created a soft, cushioned quiet reading place within a large (disused) fireplace. Here you can also 'swim upstairs' from the underwater environment of the ground floor to the first floor 'sky'. In the Children's Museum of Rhode Island, 'grandmother's kitchen' really is the kitchen of the fine Pitcher Goff Victorian mansion which houses the museum. In another room a play-house has been constructed in the style of the actual house and exhibits some of the key architectural features of the period.

Whether in a former dwelling house (Acton, Rhode Island) or fire station (Easton), in a nineteenth-century warehouse (Boston) or purpose-built modern structure (Minnesota) the important feature, common to all museums, appears to be the creation of many discrete spaces in a way that makes each space easily accessible and welcoming, but gives a sense of being in a special place apart to help children focus on the theme or topic of the exhibit. The layout must promote the feeling of exploration as you move throughout the museum, but never make it difficult or daunting to enter a particular space. On the one side is the danger of being too open, which can lead too easily to rushing about. On the other is the danger of defining the spaces so clearly that they become almost closed off.

Children's Museum of Atlanta: mission statement

To expand and enhance the opportunities metro Atlanta children have to learn by doing (interactive learning).

To operate as a museum without walls until the fund-raising climate for building a permanent facility improves.

Chesapeake Museum: mission statement

To create an environment of discovery about oneself, the peoples, the technologies and the ecology of the Chesapeake Bay area for all our children and for the child in us all.

The Discovery Museums, Acton: case study

The Discovery Museums, located in a leafy residential street in Acton, just one hour's drive from Boston, are two separate buildings and two separate, but linked, museums. The Children's Discovery Museum (CDM) opened in 1981 in a beautiful rambling Victorian dwelling house of some 3,500 square feet. The Science Discovery Museum (SDM) is a purpose-built three-level building with 6,500 square feet of exhibition space which was opened in December 1987 and is located within the grounds of the CDM house. Both museums were the brainchild of one visionary local founder who gathered around him an action group, later a board, of parents, educators, community and business leaders. The Discovery Museums Inc is a private, non-profit organisation.

The CDM is targeted primarily at toddlers and pre-school children while the SDM is designed for six to 12 year-olds. The entrance fee gives access to both museums on the one ticket.

The CDM imaginatively fits 11 theme areas into its rooms, stairway and passages. These include: dinosaurs; chain reactions; water discovery; ocean space (where children 'swim upstairs' from the ground level 'ocean floor' to the first floor 'sky'); beach space; woodland room; safari room; creative playspace (toy room and crawl space for child/parent respite and parent networking); Bessie's play diner; DUPLO room; rainbow room and the discovery ship.

The SDM is packed with hands-on exhibits designed on the principle that they 'must be interactive, open-ended, multisensory, promote adult-child interaction, and allow multiple levels of conceptual understanding'. There are 11 exhibit areas including: a pair of outside and outsize 'whisper dishes'; an earth science area; the inventors' workshop (where children noisily take apart old machines and appliances and assemble their own creations); a light and colour room; the science circus area for testing physical phenomena; a maths and topology room; an electricity room; water discovery; sound and communication; nature's balcony on the third floor and the 'tower court' which uses the full floor to cupola height of the building and includes a giant walk-through mist tornado, a large harmonograph table, 20 foot high wave-rods and a floor to ceiling chaotic pendulum.

The SDM offers 12 outreach workshop programmes to schools and runs regular scout badge workshops. Every month there is a busy programme of activities and events including story hours, family fun nights, action workshops and classes.

150,000 visitors attend the museums each year, with 10,000 students taking part in school visits and outreach sessions. Sixty per cent of visitors come from within a one hour drive of Acton. At busy times the museums have to operate a 'waiting list' system for admissions. The annual operating budget is about $800,000 of which 80% is earned from admissions, membership and outreach and workshop programmes, while 19% is fund-raised. Only 1% comes from the public sector. The Discovery Museums do not have a gift shop nor a cafeteria, but are available for birthday parties and for renting for functions and entertainments.

There are 13 full-time and 50 part-time staff and, although volunteers play an important part in the operation (1,480 hours were logged in 1994), all the floor staff in the museum are paid. The board consists of 13 members and there is an advisory board of 30 people.

The Discovery Museums emphasise that their exhibits are designed to raise questions and encourage children to go further in their own explorations. There are not always clear-cut answers – which some adults find disconcerting!

The amount of space and the shape of the premises will always determine what is possible, and for most children's museums it is a question of evolving their own character within the constraints that face them. However it is possible to identify certain key space 'ingredients' for a children's museum, in addition to the exhibition space or galleries:

- an orientation space at the entrance of the museum where there is clear signage to assist visitors in finding their way around;
- an assembly room or briefing room where school groups and other parties can be met and have their visit explained to them;
- classrooms, workshop space, activity space for both quiet and noisy sessions/classes;
- an events or performance space;

- an inside picnic area where packed lunches can be eaten;
- adequate staff facilities in addition to offices, in particular for the volunteers who make up such an important part of the staffing arrangements for most museums.
- adequate car and coach parking;
- an outside space for exhibits and events;
- a shop;
- a cafeteria.

Most museums run a shop selling mainly educational and play items, from which they earn a portion of their income. The Acton Discovery Museums, however, do not have a shop as a point of policy, not wishing to make visitors feel obliged to purchase something. For similar reasons Boston have sited their shop in such a way that visitors are not obliged to visit it, and in Minnesota the museum shop has separate access from the street and is franchised out to independent management.

Some museums run a cafeteria, others (for example Acton) do not consider it appropriate for a museum to provide food. The Children's Museum of Maine provided the space for a cafeteria in their new premises but were unable to run it successfully and are now proposing to franchise it to an external operator. Boston arranged to have McDonalds as their sub-tenant next door, on the understanding that they would introduce salads onto the menu.

Children's museums are generally open at least six days a week and often seven, although it is important to have some closed time for essential repairs, cleaning, decoration and for staff training. They are always open at the weekends and on some weekday evenings as well. When not open to the public they are frequently used for various activities and workshops or are available for hire for private functions. Most close only for a handful of national public holidays.

'To provide educational opportunities for children and their families' (Acton)

'To inspire learning through active play and exploration' (Rhode Island)

'It is a place where imagination and play are the keys to discovery. It is a place of learning and laughter. It is a place where children can come and enjoy outstanding hands-on exhibits and programs – and one another.' (Pittsburgh).

Children's museums usually receive children visitors only if they are with an adult such as a parent, carer or responsible adult bringing a group. Children's museums are not places for adults to drop off children while they go and do something else. They are based on the concept of adults and children sharing experiences and while the children are in the museum they remain entirely the responsibility of the adults with whom they came. Strict ratios are enforced, usually one adult for five children.

Untypically the Children's Museum of Maine will accept unaccompanied children, but only by prior arrangement, no more than six at any one time, with a parent or other responsible adult bringing and collecting the child and leaving them only for a specified period of time during which the parent or adult must be contactable by the museum. Exceptionally, the Brooklyn Children's Museum welcomes any children visiting without adult supervision.

Often children's museums are seen as 'safe' places where children may play without danger. In its extensive outdoor area the Bay Area Discovery Museum, San Francisco, offers children the opportunity to: 'play in streams with rocks, march in the high grass, chase each other on trails'[11] which for children in urban and suburban environments is becoming more and more limited, largely because of parental concerns over safety, injury and abduction. Thus the children's museum becomes a way in which the outdoor play an older generation took for granted may be recreated in controlled conditions.

Education

Learning is at the heart of the mission of all children's museums, expressed in a variety of ways.

Visits from schools and pre-school groups form a substantial part of the museums' visiting public (and income). Visits may be 'open' or 'focused'. Open visits are open exploration of the museum, taking advantage of whatever is happening on that day and interacting with museum staff and with the adults accompanying the group. Focused visits will include a particular hands-on activity organised and presented by the museum staff. This may be linked to the school curriculum or simply a more focused look at one facet of the museum.

The exhibits at a children's museum represent for most schools facilities which they cannot possibly replicate. Thus the museum becomes a resource to help bring alive

Intro to Homoeopathy (for parents of all ages); Toddlers Travels (2-5); How does your garden grow? (5-7); Effective discipline for parents of 2-5s (adults); Native American Spirit: stories for the family (all); Creepy Crawlers (grandparents and kids); Train club: visit to Baltimore Streetcar Museum (all); Fun and Easy science experiments (over 3); Birds of the Chesapeake Bay region (4-8); Curtain Up! (over 12); Education Rock: a family mini-concert (over 4); Toddl-art (1-3); Follow the sign (over 4). [Chesapeake]

Create a giant panda mask; build a loggerhead sea turtle; science in a box; shape your own pincushion cactus; wear you own rhinoceros horn; scuplt a clay manatee; paint a spotted jaguar face; make a black-footed ferret puppet; form a humpback whale; make a colourful birdwing butterfly; create a pop-up endangered animal card; design an camouflaged zebra; construct a lady slipper orchid. [Portsmouth]

school work. Museums provide study guides or kits for teachers so that they can both prepare for the visit and carry out follow-up work afterwards. Usually they also run teacher workshops related to the particular exhibits or themes which they are offering in the museum.

The Children's Museum of Boston lists over 100 interdisciplinary teaching units available for rent by schools and community organisations. Kits include 'educational tools – artefacts and objects, books and audiovisual materials, games, videos, and slides'.[12] The Acton Science Discovery Museum offers 12 outreach programs for schools – workshops which are delivered by museum staff. Current topics include: 'magnets; light and lasers; sound; physical changes of matter; kitchen chemistry; rocks and minerals; bubbles; static electricity; microscopes and magnification; flight; colour; pendulums'.[13] The museum runs teacher workshops 'demonstrating ways of bringing interactive education into the classroom'[14] In Boston the museum library can be freely accessed by teachers. It contains: 'an extensive collection of books, one-of-a-kind curriculum materials and multimedia resources relating to the principal themes of the museum: cultural and ethnic studies, special needs, physical and natural sciences, and child and early adolescent development'.[15]

The Children's Museum in Easton: case study

North Easton is a rural town of some 20,000 population in Massachusetts about one hour's drive from Boston. The Children's Museum (CME), which is located in a grand clapperboard Victorian fire-station building, opened in 1991 with 1,700 square feet of exhibition space.

CME was initiated by one local parent who brought together a group people all concerned to find interesting, exciting and educational things for their children to do. It took five years of planning and campaigning to get the museum open, including having to lobby for support at a town meeting to get agreement for the former fire-station to be transferred to the museum group for one dollar.

The museum serves local towns and villages up to 25 miles distant and receives 25,000 visitors per year, including 151 school groups. The target age group for CME is two to eight years.

The annual operating budget is $150,000, of which 82% is earned from admissions, membership, sales and special events. The remainder has to be fund-raised. The museum is a non-profit organisation with a Board of 10 directors who meet monthly: they include parents, teachers, social workers and people willing to fund-raise. There is also an Advisory Group of 'experts' which meets twice a year. Five staff work at the museum (three full-time), assisted by five occasional paid programme/events organisers and 25 regular volunteers.

The museum describes itself as 'a learning playground where parents and children explore, imagine, and learn about our everyday world'. The museum's exhibits include: climb the fire pole and ring the bell; roar with the dinosaurs; act it out at the performance centre; a giant kaleidoscope; blast off to the moon; and kidsclinic. There is always a changing exhibition on show throughout the museum. In May 1996 the theme was 'different cultures around the world', shortly to be replaced by 'grandparents'.

There is a continual programme of classes, workshops and activities. The Spring Sensations leaflet highlighted: dinosaur day workshop; craft workshops; Friday frolics (clay, paint, bubbles); grow a story; and after-school specials: animal action; colours and shapes; people and places; body basics; world of action; earth and sky, maths marvels. The summer 'camp' was being advertised and the second annual five mile race. A pre-school playgroup runs one day a week and the museum is available for birthday parties, 'sleep-overs' and private parties.

CME has been raising funds to develop the basement of its building and was hoping to start work on site in summer 1996. The basement will provide additional activity space, an indoor picnic area and space for quiet programmes.

The museum considers its primary audience to be families, not just children, and recognises that adults need to learn something too from their visits. An interactive parent/child relationship is encouraged.

Following the success of the Children's Museum the town 'Selectmen' (local council) has asked it to expand its target age-range to include teenagers up to 15 years. CME is considering this but recognises that such a development will require a separate facility in a separate building.

Museums play a role not only in complementing what can be done in schools, but also in offering training for teachers and becoming involved in curriculum development. Boston, for example, is involved with a collaborative project aimed at helping teachers achieve changes in the attitudes of young people towards science studies.

The Children's Museum of Rhode Island emphasises the importance of its outreach programmes for schools as a means of getting the museum experience to children in low income areas. It reports how a majority of its visitors to the museum are middle-class and English-spoken and yet in the inner-city areas of the State capital city, Providence, English is today the native tongue of no more than 30% of the population. It is to these non-English speaking communities that they seek to deliver their outreach programmes. To do this it is necessary to raise specific funding to cover the costs.

On-site activities

Children's museums are much more than places to go and experience the hands-on exhibits. They are centres for a wide range of activities and programmes, going on during the day, in the evenings and at weekends.

The May Highlights at the very small Chesapeake Children's Museum illustrate the extent of activities and the breadth of target audiences, as do the June 'dates to remember' at the Portsmouth Children's Museum (New Hampshire).

Museums run after-school clubs and pre-school mornings. They offer Scout Badge workshops. Most hold special holiday events, especially in the summer, which they call 'camps'. These are events to which children may go unaccompanied, but are not residential, except perhaps for the occasional 'sleep-over'. The themes of the Richmond Children's Museum's six-week 'City Slickers Summer Camp' were: painting, sculpture, photography and craft work; 'touring the world'; nature and wildlife exploration; local 'history mysteries'; backstage at a local theatre; on and by the river.

Museums usually offer a birthday party package: a party room with a special cake and other treats, perhaps a special activity and free-range of the museum for the party group. Most museums also offer 'sleep-overs': the chance to camp out in the children's museum in your favourite exhibit area and to enjoy a special activity in the evening. The facilities of the museums, outside public opening hours, are marketed for cultural events, private parties and even for business functions.

Museums find themselves, or put themselves, at the centre of local fun events. Boston brings the Big Apple Circus to the city. Richmond organises an annual soap box derby which is run down a hill in the centre of the city: 51 races for drivers between the ages of nine and 16 years. Easton runs a five mile road race each year – fun and fund-raising for the museum at the same time!

Outreach and other programmes

Children's museums are not just about being visited; many have travelling exhibits available for hire and most have some pro-active policy of taking exhibits to the community, and not just to schools or other educational establishments. For some, this outreach work *is* the museum. The Children's Museum of Acadiana functioned without premises for eight years, taking its exhibits out to a range of community venues, including shopping malls and community festivals.

The Children's Museum of Atlanta, operating without walls until 'the fund-raising climate for building a permanent facility improves' has developed what it calls its 'exhibience' programme which:

> 'uses the best elements of children's exhibits and youth museum experiences in community classrooms and neighbourhoods. Thematic in nature, an Exhibience uses artefacts, exhibits, and simulations and incorporates elements of the following in a total interactive learning experience: handicrafts, multisensory

Miami Youth Museum: mission statement

The Miami Youth Museum is a non-profit educational institution. We open our doors to children of all ages, their families, childcare providers and educators for multisensory, participatory discovery. The museum offers exhibitions, programs and learning materials related to the arts, sciences, history, humanities, careers and life-experiences.

MYM provides opportunities to meet the needs of children of all socioeconomic, physical, emotional and educational levels in our multi-ethnic community. The Museum's sensitivity to and knowledge of South Florida's multicultural audience is reflected in our staff composition, exhibition content and programming. Visitors are encouraged to make choices, imagine, create, pretend and play together. The Miami Youth Museum is dedicated to enriching children's lives by fostering a love of learning and an appreciation of their own unique talents and skills.

experiences, gross motor activity, visual and performing arts, and technology.'[16]

Museums may also become involved in projects and programmes which address specific needs within the community. The Children's Museum of Boston defines outreach 'as a way to extend programmes to low-income people and communities of color' and in the 1970s created a Community Services Division and hired staff to work with community agencies 'almost exclusively at community sites to develop arts, science and early childhood activities'.[17] Museum staff have also been involved in neighbourhood festivals and events. Special transport is arranged for 'community nights' at the museum.

Currently the Children's Museum of Boston is involved with other organisations in the Boston area with a Families First Parenting Program. This takes the form of a Parent Resource Center within the museum next to the Playspace exhibit (for toddlers), a programme of workshops and access to counselling and consultation. In Rhode Island the Children's Museum runs a 'Families Together' programme for court-separated families and intact families in need of guidance. Visits to the museum under the guidance of a family therapist on the staff of the museum offer opportunities for family interaction and bonding. Families benefiting from the programme are referred by social service agencies.

Programmes for teenagers

The role for teens in children's museums is usually to become volunteer staff. The Children's Museum of Maine organises its young volunteer help into three categories of experience and expertise: 'discoverers', 'explorers' and 'engineers'. Children can become 'discoverers' from the age of 10 years. These young volunteers receive in-house training and are programmed into the staffing schedule of the museum. They also join with paid staff in training and planning sessions.

The Brooklyn Children's Museum runs a Museum Team Program, starting with the 'Kids Crew' of volunteers-in-training who, when they become fully-fledged volunteers, can graduate to a paid internship during which they will receive career counselling, job search assistance, help with applying to college, and time and money management skills.

However, some museums do offer specific exhibits or programmes for the over-12s. Boston currently has a 'Teen Tokyo' exhibit which introduces US youth to the life of teenagers in Japan through common interests such as music, sports, fashion, school and family life. Chesapeake offers drama work for the over-12s and Easton has been asked by the Town Council to consider setting up a project for local teenagers. The museum managers, while considering this, are very clear that for such a project to be successful it requires to be run as a discrete project, separate from the Children's Museum and with the full involvement of the teenagers themselves.

Staffing: paid and unpaid

Children's museums are labour-intensive institutions and the larger ones employ significant numbers of people. The Children's Museum of Boston, for example,

Children's Museum of Maine: mission statement

The mission of the Children's Museum of Maine is to facilitate and to enhance the learning and curiosity of children and adults through the exploration of the arts, humanities, nature and science. To this purpose, the museum provides exhibits, programs, and outreach in a safe, nurturing environment. The museum strives to be sensitive and respectful of the diversity of children's backgrounds and languages, as well as their intrinsic creative knowledge to speak for themselves and their world.

currently has 125 employees (it has been as high as 160 in the past) of whom 75 are full-time. These are organised into six functional departments: Programme and Evaluation; Education; Visitor Services; Public Relations and Marketing; Human Resources; and Development. The Children's Museum of Indianapolis has 180 full-time and 200 part-time staff organised into 11 sections: Education; Exhibits; Visitor Services; Administration/Operations; Volunteers; Membership; Marketing/Development; Museum Shop; Public Relations; Human Resources; and Programs. By contrast Chesapeake has one paid post shared by five people, while Easton has three full-time and two part-time staff, with five occasional consultants to run specific programmes.

Children's museum staff, especially in the larger and longer-established museums, are very much career professionals and the scale of the children's museum sector in the United States permits career-improving moves to be made within the sector. The bi-monthly *AYM News* runs classified advertisements for museum staff, and its 'personnel changes' column regularly records such career moves. There is also significant career interchange between the children's museums and other institutions in the museum and gallery world.

In the museum continuum, children's museums blur almost seamlessly into the traditional sector. Near the point of intersection it is difficult to distinguish the types, but probably it does not matter. What is significant are the career opportunities which are offered, and the possibilities for setting up training programmes which offer young people real job prospects throughout the children's and the traditional museum worlds.

In all children's museums, large and small, the enthusiasm and commitment of the staff is palpable and infectious. Yet all depend on the unpaid help of volunteers. The Discovery Museums in Acton logged 1,480 hours of volunteer work in 1994 while Rhode Island recorded a contribution of over 7,000 hours from 200 volunteers. Indianapolis lists 1,575 volunteers supporting its paid staff.

The Discovery Museums, Acton: mission statement

To provide educational opportunities for children and their families to explore and make discoveries about themselves and their world with emphasis on natural settings, physical sciences, arts, humanities and enjoyable creative activities that will contribute to the growth and development of children.

The Children's Museum of Rhode Island: case study

CMRI is located in an historic Victorian Pitcher Goff town house in Pawtucket, part of the conurbation surrounding the State capital of Providence. The house was obtained on a generous lease from the Congregational Church in return for its renovation. The museum opened its 5,000 square feet in 1977 after two years of fund-raising by local parents and teachers and much DIY labour to refurbish the building and build the exhibits.

The museum is targeted at children up to 11 years old and has nine exhibit areas: the State Room (which includes a giant 'play-on' map of Rhode Island and a history room complete with colonial costumes to try on and a revolutionary war sailing boat); my way, your way (about disabilities); sea-o-rama; our house (a playsize version of the museum house with architectural detail); great grandmother's kitchen and pantry; Estella the superchairwoman (who gives you a big hug); story makers; the shape lab; and Presto Change-oh! (where you can create murals and experiment with design).

CMRI has two travelling exhibits in its 'museum on wheels': You too? about the human body, and Magic Words, a literacy outreach programme. A full calendar of school focus visits is offered and there is a regular public programme on Wednesdays and Sundays and a pre-school programme every Friday. The May 1996 schedule included: rhyme time; story-telling; celebrate Mom!; stories by multimedia; family fun day; beautiful bugs and 'scienterrific'. The museum runs a special Families Together Programme which offers supported visits and counselling to court-separated families and others needing help.

CMRI occasionally commissions special works of art for children from professional artists and these are displayed in the museum. It also keeps small permanent collections: hand-crafted marionettes; dolls and toys from the late-nineteenth to mid-twentieth century; miniature buildings; and period postcards and pictures relating to the museum building.

The annual attendance is about 50,000 people, of whom 80% are from Rhode Island State. At peak times the museum has to implement a 'waiting line' for admissions as it is restricted to a maximum of 120 visitors at any time. The annual operating budget is $400,000, of which 50% is earned and 50% fund-raised or contributed as grants. The museum has a strong policy of ensuring that people are not debarred from attending because of cost. One Sunday a month is free entry and free passes are given out liberally, such that 30% of admissions do not pay. There is a small museum shop.

Twelve full-time and three part-time staff work for the museum. There are 200 volunteers on the books of whom 40-50 are active at any one time. A board of 30 directors has fund-raising as its most important task. *Ad hoc* advisory committees are set up to assist with particular issues or projects, such as the content and design of a new exhibit.

By 1997 CMRI plans to have moved to new premises in downtown Providence, to a converted 1939 factory in the 'jewelry district' which will give 15,000 square feet of museum space as well as adequate parking and an outdoor area for exhibits and events. In particular the new museum will provide 'an orientation space' on arrival; an assembly room for school briefings, for eating packed lunches and so on (at present all this has to happen on the school buses); adequate storage facilities for collections and exhibits not in use; staff facilities, especially for the floor staff. The new building will be fully accessible to people with disabilities. The capital campaign for the new building, well on the way to completion, is $3m.

In order to recruit, sift, train and programme such large amounts of volunteer help, most museums will have a volunteer co-ordinator as a full-time paid member of staff. Most also report the usual problems with using volunteers – being certain that you have the right number (with the right skills) at the right time, and coping with the inevitable problems that arise when a volunteer does not turn up.

The work that volunteers might do will vary from museum to museum. The volunteer recruitment leaflet put out by the Children's Museum of South Eastern Connecticut distinguishes between tasks which require audience contact and those which do not, recognising that prospective volunteers will have varying skills and inclinations. Under the former heading they list 'arts and crafts aides; explainers/docents; program teachers; audience aides', and under the latter 'bulk mailings; clerical/office work; exhibit construction; facilities maintenance; fund-raising and membership; research and collections'. They emphasise that 'volunteers at this museum are treated like the professionals they are and will be fully trained by the museum staff to ensure that everyone is comfortable with the tasks at hand'. The benefits of being a volunteer include free passes to the museum and a discount in the museum shop. There is also an annual 'Volunteer Recognition Week' during which the work and achievements of the volunteers are publicly recognised and celebrated.[18]

Museums also tap into various programmes in order to increase their pool of staff without incurring staff costs. These programmes include students on work placement (usually from teacher-training or childcare courses), students doing community service through the Americorps scheme and work experience schemes.

All museums emphasise the vital importance of the 'floor staff' – those people who are in the museum dealing with visitors whenever it is open, the people on whom the atmosphere and style of the museum experience depend. Their name varies: 'interpreters'; 'explainers'; 'monitors'; but the task is key. Boston describes it as 'drawing visitors into the exhibits and providing a more in-depth understanding of the content'.[19] Acton talks about 'a questioning mode of interaction' and defines four main functions: leading with questions; helping kids engage; dealing with inappropriate behaviour; keeping the place clean and tidy. All the floor staff at Acton are paid in order to ensure quality and reliability. In other museums floor staff are often likely to be students or on work placement, or may be volunteers.

The training of staff, whether paid or volunteer, is an important part of the running of any children's museum and especially for the floor staff. Equally important is to find space for staff to meet and rest when off the floor – sometimes not so high a priority when space demands are tight.

Organisational structure

The majority of children's museums are incorporated as private, non-profit, tax-exempt organisations – essentially the United States equivalent of a British company limited by guarantee and registered as a charity. Exceptionally (the Garden State Discovery Museum, New Jersey for example) a museum may be formed as a for-profit business and others might be run as part of the local authority. The Children's Museum of Virginia, which was formed originally as a community project in 1980, was taken into Portsmouth City Council's Department of Museums in 1982 and now is one of four museums run by the Department.

The boards (the trustees) of the private, non-profit organisations are self-appointing bodies, brought together initially by the founding person or persons and may range in size from 10 to over 30 members. A board will try and ensure that it is broadly representative of the local community it serves – by race and by culture; that it is balanced as regards gender; and that it has within it the sort of expertise and experience needed by the organisation such as work with children; social services; education; legal matters; business management; fund-raising.

Such a self-appointing board, which is accountable to the community and to other constituencies by custom and practice rather than by democracy, can be, and often is, very responsive and accountable, not least because the organisation depends on local goodwill and support to survive. But at the end of the day it is fundamentally exclusive rather than inclusive and there is little evidence in the United States of children and young people being involved in the governance of the museums.

It is not always easy to recruit a diverse board and the Children's Museum of Boston suggests:

'If you are having trouble finding people from diverse backgrounds who want to participate as board members, it may be helpful to set up a focus group or speak directly with several community leaders to better understand the real or perceived barriers.'[20]

It emphasises diversity 'in terms of gender, racial and ethnic composition, urban/suburban, class and occupation'[21] and the need to ensure not only that there is system of 'board turnover' but that the process is well-known and understood, and therefore more likely to be used.

The initial board of a museum in the process of starting up will be the group who have come together to plan and create it. They will most likely do everything: lobby, fund-raise, build exhibits, publicise, staff it and so on. As the museum evolves and matures, acquiring staff, the role of the board necessarily changes to that of policy review, guidance for the director and staff and, especially, fund-raising. Not surprisingly this change can be difficult for long-standing board members, who were in at the beginning, to come to terms with. It may also be difficult for newer directors to build up the same commitment. Museum professionals report problems both with board members who will not 'let go' to staff and with those who remain reluctant to convert their general interest into an active support role. Fund-raising, and the maintenance of key local relationships, seem to be the most important roles of board members in an established museum.

Museums will often establish some form of advisory board which meets less frequently than the management board and which is used both to access professional expertise of relevance to the museum's work (in particular educationalists, child development specialists, other museum professionals) and to associate a wide range of such professionals with the museum and its work. Some may form instead *ad hoc* advisory groups for specific purposes such as developing a particular exhibit or advising on personnel matters. The Children's Museum of Maine forms departmental advisory committees which bring together staff, both paid and unpaid, with board members and outside 'experts'.

Membership of a children's museum does not confer any rights in governance. Membership subscriptions give the right of admission to the museum and access to other services.

Getting started: establishing a museum

The most common way for a children's museum to start up is through the energy of a group of people, usually white and middle class, who determine to do as others have done and create a children's museum for their children within their community. Often, there is a key charismatic or dynamic person who leads this innovative process. Such was the case in Acton (see panel on page 51) and in Easton it was Paula Peterson, a parent of three boys who was toiling to find creative and engaging things for them to do. She brought together a group of four local parents – a banker, a public administrator, a writer and an events organiser – to plot and develop the children's museum idea. It took them five years of planning and development time to achieve their goal, in the course of which they had to go to a town meeting to persuade the population that they, and their plans, were sufficiently competent for the disused Victorian fire station building in the town to be sold to them at a peppercorn price of one dollar. This was a decision which the town's board of 'Selectmen' (council) was not competent to approve without the ratification of a full town meeting. After they had publicised their ideas and lobbied for support, a public meeting attended by 700 townspeople endorsed their plans.

The Junior League, a women's organisation which aims to serve the local community, has often been the focus for first discussions about planning a new children's museum. When the Children's Museum of Maine first opened in 1977 its entire first year operating budget was funded from the sales of a thrift shop run by the Junior League. They took it one year at a time to start with: 'The only way to overcome our

The Acton museums

'The Discovery Museums, the Science and the Children's Museums, are the babies of Acton resident Donald Verger, a math teacher and naturalist. After Verger became a new parent, he decided young children need a place for interactive and educational experiences in MetroWest. Along with a board of community leaders, Verger founded the Children's Museum which opened in October 1981 in a 100 year-old Victorian house. The museum proved popular but as his kids grew, Verger decided the next step was to develop a hands-on science museum for kids aged six and over where multi-disciplinary learning combines math, science and art. The Science Discovery Museum, built behind the Children's Museum, opened in December 1987'.[22]

insecurity, our hesitancy, was to set it up as a demonstration project. We did it on a strictly volunteer basis at first. We hired the first (paid) director much later, when it became clear it was going to succeed.'[23]

The planning phase for a museum will vary according to local circumstances, but it is not unusual for the planning and development phase to take several years. The average planning time of 75 museums responding to the AYM 1996 survey was 3.01 years.

As museums mature, grow and require more substantial premises they may become part of the process of downtown (inner city) revitalisation. In Portland, Maine, the Children's Museum received financial support from the council in order to move into the chamber of commerce building in the city centre. In this location, next to the Museum of Fine Art, the Children's Museum is a key feature in the plan to transform the waterfront heart of the city. Similarly, the new children's museum building in Portsmouth, Virginia was developed by the city in 1993-4 as part of its waterfront revitalisation programme. In St Paul, Minnesota, the new Children's Museum has been developed as part of a programme to revive the downtown and build up a range of cultural and entertainment venues. To this end the museum received the site and three million dollars towards its capital programme from the city authorities.

Community involvement

Although membership of a children's museum does not give any rights of governance, the very nature of the institutions and what they do – recreational and educational programmes meeting social needs, generating fun – involves a wide range of people in every aspect of the museum's day-to-day life.

Where they are formed through a 'bottom-up' process (and by far the greatest number are formed in this way) the very process of formation is involving and will succeed only if the founding group is able to build up the support it needs from local institutions: the council, business people, the museum and gallery community, schools and the local education world, social service organisations, and of course from their target public: children and the parents of young children. It is these strong local roots which both sustain the museum as a social enterprise and give it its direction and legitimacy to serve the community.

The management boards and the advisory boards contain a cross-section of community interests and thus involve quite large numbers of people in the museum in a serious way. The Children's Museum of Boston has a board of 38 trustees and a board of 75 overseers (advisers). The Discovery Museums in Acton have a (relatively) smallish management board of 13 but an advisory board of 30. Rhode Island has 33 members on its management board and a wide range of people involved from time to time on its *ad hoc* advisory groups. When those involved in a management and advisory capacity are aggregated with staff, volunteers and other regular helpers, even the smallest museums are regularly drawing on the services of many people to keep the institution going.

Fund-raising necessarily brings museums into close contact with those whom they are asking for contributions and involves people not only in giving but sometimes in more energetic participation, such as the Easton fun-run.

The AYM statistics record that a total of 9,297,543 people visited 85 museums in 1995, giving an average per museum of 109,383.[24] 25,000 visit Easton each year while 400,000 visit Boston. Outreach activities add to these figures; indeed, in the case of Boston it is estimated that the outreach and community programmes bring the museum into contact annually with another 250,000 people. Paid-up museum memberships range from 700 in Easton, through 2,300 in Rhode Island to 13,421 in Indianapolis. Visitors, especially members, tend to make repeated visits.

As another mechanism to involve people most museums provide a suggestions box or a 'talk-back' board as a means of seeking the views of visitors and enabling customers to contribute their ideas and comments. From observation these boards are both well and valuably used.

Children's Museum of Maine: case study

When the Children's Museum of Maine (CMM) first opened in 1977 it was based in an empty school building, was run by Junior League members (a women's service organisation) and funded through thrift shop sales. The stimulus for the women was 'a desire to have something for the children of Portland that would be a hands-on learning experience similar to the Children's Museum of Boston'. By 1980 the museum had become an independent organisation located in a 4,000 square feet Victorian house, but it was not until 1986 that it hired its first paid member of staff.

By 1993 the museum had relocated to newly refurbished premises 'smack dab in downtown Portland': the fine former Chamber of Commerce building next door to the Museum of Art. The new children's museum provides 9,000 square feet of exhibition space in a 17,500 square feet building, developed for a capital cost of $2.5m.

All the exhibits are Maine made: devised, designed and constructed locally. They include: a stalactite cave; fire engine; lobster boat; supermarket; bank complete with a working 'hole in wall' machine that delivers CMM currency; farmyard corner; space shuttle; a giant revolving globe; cycling skeleton; news centre with TV monitors and cameras; weather and geography station; a planetarium; jigsaw puzzle map of the United States; and a range of science exhibits, including Bernoulli Blowers, magnet tables, balls and cranks, Archimedes screw. There is also a 'toddler park', a science bar where experiments can be done by small groups and a fully equipped computer room with some 20 keyboards and monitors. At the top of the building is a cupola with a state of the art camera obscura, donated by Eastman Kodak, which offers a fantastic 360° panoramic view of Portland.

The Museum includes a regularly changing special exhibit: autumn 1995 was 'Pyramid Power'; spring 1996 'Bug Builders'. Special classroom activity packs are prepared to go with these exhibitions as well as school programmes and teacher workshops at the museum. The May 1996 programme of general activities listed: family learning days; a clean-up crew for the museum; talking to animals; photo exhibition; astronomy day; mask making; an old-fashioned games party; magic attic doll club; a narrow gauge train; fist printing; spring crafts;

toddlers' mornings; light and the camera obscura; pee wee art; dinosaurs; fossil club; insect art adventures. The two week 'summer camp' will take the form of a nineteenth-century railroad car at the museum for 'train tales, train lore and hands-on locomotion fun'.

There is a board of 22 directors, whose role has changed over time. Originally the founders did everything: planned the museum, designed and built the exhibits, ran the place. Now the role of the board is more to do with fund-raising and general guidance than with hands-on involvement.

There are 14 museum staff, supported by around 50 volunteers, students and people on work placement schemes. The museum runs a programme to encourage teenagers to work as volunteer staff and between 10 and 15 are scheduled into the daily roster and are included in staff training sessions. About 120,000 people visit the museum each year and the operating budget is $800,000 of which approximately 70% is earned income.

CMM is conscious of the need to reach out to the low-income sections of the community and seeks to build up partnerships with youth groups in the city.

The influence of children and young people

Children's museums, however child-centred, are essentially institutions with a pedagogical purpose, whose exhibits and programmes are determined by adults. Their style emphasises involvement, seeking feedback to ensure that the child customers are well served and satisfied with the product and the service.

Usually exhibits will be tested out at the planning and prototype stages to see how children react to them. Some museums use focus groups to seek the ideas and views of their young customers. The 'talk-back' boards provide a mechanism for comment. Floor staff are encouraged to facilitate this process as well as to listen and observe the reactions of the children. Museums also conduct formal and informal evaluations of exhibits and of programmes but, for the most part, this will take the form of consulting teachers and group leaders, rather than directly consulting the child customers.

There will tend to be a greater level of involvement by young people over the age of 12 at the point where the teenagers, when they become volunteer staff, begin to participate in the running of the museum and take part in training. Where museums have programmes for teenagers, they are likely to set up some form of advisory

The Children's Museum, Boston: mission statement

The Children's Museum in Boston exists to help children understand and enjoy the world in which they live.

As an early museum experience for children, the environment at the Children's Museum is informal, but its purpose is serious. Central to the Museum's philosophy is the belief that real objects, direct experiences and enjoyment support learning. To involve all kinds of learners, a variety of strategies and programs are used.

Children should grow up feeling secure and self-confident with respect for others and the natural world. The Museum encourages imagination, curiosity, questioning and realism; it provides opportunities for new insights, involvement with the world and understanding of human differences.

The Children's Museum is committed to:

- serving a culturally and economically diverse audience, primarily from the Greater Boston area, but also from New England and throughout the country;
- creating exhibitions and programs which provide thought-provoking interactions with real objects in the areas of cultural understanding, science and human development;
- maintaining cultural and natural history collections at the highest museum standards and making them accessible to a broad public;
- attracting and supporting a diverse staff who share a commitment to children and bring creativity and expertise to the work of the Museum;
- providing resources and support for parents;
- working with teachers and community agency staff to extend the Museum's philosophy and resources;
- serving as a national research and development centre continually exploring new methods of informal education, as well as new roles for museums.

group. Thus the Children's Museum of Maine has a Youth Advisory Board and the Children's Museum of Boston has had teenage advisory groups in the past, although no longer since it re-focused its work onto the under-12s.

Questions of money

Just over half of the museums responding to the 1996 AYM survey are more than 50% financially self-sustaining and 11% are more than 90% self-sustaining from earned income. Earned income includes admissions, membership fees, shop sales, rentals (lettings, birthday parties, sleep-overs, etc) and contracts (for specific services provided such as the Families Together programme in Rhode Island). Other sources of (unearned) income are: grants from the public sector (federal, state and local council), fund-raising and income from investments and endowments. Sums that are fund-raised each year are often included within the earned income category, presumably on the grounds that a great deal of work goes into the activities which raise it and that it is thus truly 'earned'!

Raising funds is a continuous process. Probably in the United States there is a stronger tradition of local fund-raising and an expectation that the way to do things locally is to create an organisation, raise the money and get on and do it. Equally there is an easier tolerance of a mix of earned and unearned income to sustain a social enterprise.

The average entrance fee (1996) for children's museums was $3.38 for a child and $3.66 for an adult (senior citizen $3.34).[25] Many museums will admit children under two years free of charge and all run membership schemes which give families unlimited admittance to the museum for an annual payment in the range $35 to $75.

The AYM runs a reciprocal membership scheme to which some 50 children's museums throughout the United States belong. For a payment of a minimum $100 to their local children's museum, a family of four can have free admission to all the museums taking part in the scheme and receive the same admission privileges as are accorded to local members. In New England, where there are some 10 children's museums within a two-hour drive of each other, it is possible for families to make regular use of this scheme to give their children a very wide range of museum experiences.

Serving the under-served

Most museums are very aware of the risk of denying the museum experience to families on low incomes because of the cost of admission and take various steps to try and ensure that the 'under-served' are in fact served. Door and desk staff in

photo: John Pearce

The Amazing Space, an entirely 'commercial children's museum', located in the Mall of America, Minnesota, describes itself as 'Presenting a space where fun meets learning, children's museum meets movie and adult meets child in surprising new ways'.

57

Boston are trained to watch for families who may arrive and baulk at the admission price and turn away. In this situation staff will make contact outside the museum and seek to negotiate a compromise, which may involve a price reduction or a deal whereby the family undertakes to do some volunteer work. Friday evenings at the Boston museum are free.

Similarly the Discovery Museums in Acton claim never to turn anyone away because they cannot afford the entrance price. They too will try and negotiate a deal, while always expecting the family or group to pay something. Indeed it is usually to ensure that groups from low-income areas can attend that special arrangements have to be made. These may take the form of seeking corporate sponsorship for visits or specific grant aid from the local council.

The Children's Museum of Rhode Island admits everyone free of charge on the first Sunday of each month and has a policy of giving out free passes to families and groups whom they wish to encourage to attend and whom they believe may not be able to afford to. Thus over 30% of their admissions are free.

Viability

The dilemma for all children's museums, as for any enterprise with social aims, is to ensure that there is sufficient income to sustain the project financially while at the same time achieving the maximum possible social impact. It is what Lou Casagrande, director of the Children's Museum in Boston, calls a 'two lobe job', as explained in the museum's house magazine:

> 'While competition for the dollar has become a fact of life for Children's Museum management, Casagrande sees himself and the museum first as educators working with kids and the community, and second as entrepreneurs aiming to maximize their resources. Though healthy cash flow keeps the organisation healthy, it is programmes that keep it vital. "Our members and visitors and the community judge us not by how much we make," he says, "but by how much good we do with each dollar."'[26]

Regardless of the actual mix of earned and unearned income, children's museums require to be run in a businesslike fashion in order to survive and to be efficient. That means adopting best business practice and using it to the benefit of the museum, an approach described with some verve in the booklet *Non profit piggy goes to market* about the approach adopted at the Denver Children's Museum in the late 1970s:

> 'We not only manage the museum like a business; we are a business. We are in the business of running an educational, participatory museum for children, and of producing high quality educational products for families. Our marketing strategy does not interfere with our educational goals: it enhances them and allows us to reach more of our constituents at little or no cost to them or to the museum.'[27]

No matter how businesslike the approach, for the majority of children's museums the reality is that some funds have to be raised each year, a task which consumes time and energy. The trend is one of reducing public sector support and finding ways of earning or raising more income or converting to a contract basis the services that were previously funded by annual grants.

Some of the larger and older museums have acquired endowment capital which gives them a regular annual income and a number are exploring how to seek further endowments. Local companies and other businesses have played and will continue to play an important part in resourcing the children's museums, either by direct financial assistance or through help in kind. And all museums publish their 'wish list' in their newsletters or other publications, putting out calls for what they need and what members of the local community may be able to donate.

Competition

Children's museums are increasingly having to compete not only with other museums and galleries but also with the commercial world of visitor centres where 'infotainment' and 'edutainment' mix entertainment and fun with learning something and with commercial 'pay for play' provision.

The Amazing Space is a 'commercial children's museum' which opened in May 1996 in the Mall of America, close by the twin towns of St Paul and Minneapolis in Minnesota. Advertising as 'Where Dr Spock meets Dr Seuss' it describes the facility as 'Presenting a space where fun meets learning, children's museum meets movie and adult meets child in surprising new ways'.[28] The Amazing Space is an entirely commercial operation in America's largest shopping mall. While the emphasis is on the concept, usual in children's museums, of adults visiting with children, it is possible to drop off children, with a system of electronic security wristbands to ensure that the right children are reunited with the right adults. Its target market is school, daycare and other groups as well as individual families.

Despite the competition, children's museums in the United States continue to grow in number and in size because they are much more than either a hands-on experience or a childcare facility. They are centres for children and families, for learning and play, for community activities, for engagement between generations; they are built on significant community involvement and respond to the needs of the community in which they are based and which they seek to serve. Each children's museum develops its role or market niche in the community in relation to what already exists, and with the general presumption that it will seek to serve all sections of the community. The children's museum may function like a business, but at its heart it is a community project, rooted in the community and working for the benefit of all children in the community.

Children's museums in the United States are a movement with a sense of purpose and excitement. What comes with that is a willingness to share and to help others to follow in their footsteps. Although they adopt a commercial approach, as does any social enterprise and community organisation in the 1990s, they seem to eschew the secrecy which often goes with the marketplace approach. Existing museums are ready and willing to help others join the movement and do the same.

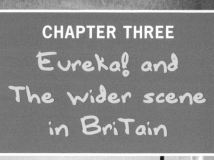

CHAPTER THREE

Eureka! and The wider scene in BriTain

photo: Eureka! The Museum for Children

'Playful' self-instruction is in fact the hall mark of the enquiring mind, and, as all great teachers have understood, the art of education lies mainly in the stage-management of a situation so that children are enabled to learn for themselves. *John and Elizabeth Newsom*[1]

I hear and I forget,
I see and I remember,
I do and I understand. *Ancient Chinese proverb*[2]

This chapter describes Eureka! The Museum for Children based in Halifax, Yorkshire which is the only institution in Britain describing itself as a children's museum in the US sense. The chapter also briefly identifies and surveys some of the other organisations and institutions in Britain whose work and activities encompass some of the characteristics of a children's museum.

The Children's Experience Centre

The origins of Eureka!, which was opened by the Prince of Wales in Halifax in July 1992, go back to 1980 when a London community worker, Rosemary Goldsmith, coming across children's museums in the United States, asked the question: 'Why haven't we got one in London?' She put together a steering group of people interested in the idea and formed a charitable company, 'The Children's Experience Centre Limited' (CEC). The idea was to combine some of the best features of British primary education with the best developments of the North American children's museums.

Their objectives were ambitious (see panel on page 64) and their ambition for the company was high. The centre was to 'be the first of many, both in the United Kingdom and overseas. Future growth of the new company will come through expansion of the first centre, development of new centres and the franchising of the know-how, systems and designs.'[3]

By 1982 the CEC had persuaded the Department of Trade and Industry to give a development grant of £50,000 and it was possible to commission design consultants, who made a study tour to North America, and to commission a viability study from the English Tourist Board. An advisory panel of educationalists and psychologists was created to guide and comment on the work of the design team.

The Children's Experience Centre: objectives

'To create a wide range of interactive exhibits and activities, including the arts and humanities but centering on science, engineering and technology, with an emphasis on the most advanced developments and on information technology. These will let the child explore actively and think creatively; the wind tunnel, TV studio, laserium, computer and robotics sections will capture and hold the visiting child's imagination.

'To design the Centre using the concepts that have been highly successful in other technologically advanced countries, notably the United States and in Belgium, Japan, Israel and the Netherlands.

'To equip, staff and service the Centre specifically for the needs of children in Great Britain of all inclinations and abilities, including the handicapped, enabling them to 'learn by doing' about the working world around them.

'To establish an important educational resource for schools in the vital fields of science and technology.

'To create a major tourist attraction in London that will provide an educational leisure facility for children and their families.

'To design and present exhibits so that they will be within the understanding of under-11 year-olds, although there will be no age limit for visitors – ensuring that labelling is clear, simple and at child height and that specially trained staff, who will attend each exhibit, encourage, explain and help.

'To make available a wide range of back-up services including special services for schools, evaluation and monitoring, a shop selling computers and software and learning resource kits, workshop events and a themed cafeteria with child appeal.

'To help children towards an enthusiastic and imaginative response to science and technology, building a vital learning base for the social and industrial growth of Great Britain.'[4]

By 1984 there was a detailed proposal and business plan, which envisaged a CEC of some 25,000 square feet with 16,000 square feet of exhibition space. The proposed layout included an entrance with interactive sound and light displays, a production line, a laserium, a wind tunnel, a TV studio, an 'all about me' exhibit, body movement, car movement, robotics, and a sectioned house. There would also be a shop, café area and picnic space. The business plan envisaged that on a visitor attendance of 360,000 the CEC would be not only viable, but profitable.

Eureka!

At this point the initiative stalled, largely on the twin issues of finding suitable premises and potential investors. In 1985 the interest of Vivien Duffield of the Vivien Duffield Foundation was engaged. She effectively took the initiative over, forming a new Children's Museum charitable organisation and appointing a new set of trustees.

Nonetheless the initiative continued to stall on the question of finding suitable premises in London until in 1987, the alternative of Halifax was suggested by the Prince of Wales. It was still not until 1989, however, that the Halifax site was confirmed; but by then serious planning for the first children's museum in Britain was underway. That planning, development and construction stage would still require three and a half years before the museum was ready to open.

The Halifax site is a former railway goods yard of some 12.5 acres and was in the ownership of the local authority (Calderdale). The council's major contribution to the project has been a 125-year lease at minimal cost for the site, which is adjacent to the railway station and very near the town centre. It had to obtain special permission from the Secretary of State to arrange this lease rather than sell the site at open market valuation.

By far the greatest part of the £8.5m capital required to develop Eureka! has come from the Vivien Duffield Foundation and its associated Clore Foundation. Mrs Duffield was also able to bring on board the active support of a group of local Halifax businessmen, putting in place the third of the three key factors: a site, sufficient capital and local support. It was thus that Eureka! 'descended on Halifax like a white tornado' as one consultee expressed it.

Eureka describes itself as:

> 'the first museum of its kind in the UK ... wholly designed to teach children up to the age of 12 about themselves and the world in which we live, using a hands-on, fun approach to learning and development. At Eureka! children are actively encouraged to touch, listen and smell as well as look, and share their discoveries with adults.'[5]

There are over 400 exhibits which have been developed in consultation with children and teachers and 'creatively designed using the latest technology to encourage the enquiring mind and facilitate learning by discovery'.[6]

The exhibits

The exhibits are arranged in four main themed areas:[7]

Me and my body is introduced by Scoot, the talking robot, who encourages children to increase their knowledge of themselves by using the exhibits to discover how the body and the five different senses work. Children can step inside a giant mouth to find the wobbly tooth, play pinball digestion and learn how joints and muscles work by riding the skeleton bike. In this exhibition area visitors can also find out how the choices we make affect our well-being and experience what it is like to have a disability.

Living and working together provides an environment where children can become a member of an extended family as well as part of modern day society. Visitors can unfold the mysteries and complexities of daily life as they explore the group of buildings around the Town Square which include a house, shop, bank, garage, factory and petrol filling station.

Money can be printed, withdrawn or deposited at the Eureka! bank, the week's shopping can be selected and paid for in the mini Marks & Spencer food hall, while letters and parcels can be sorted at the Post Office and delivered around the square, where there is also a dig, a fountain and a gigantic story tree.

Invent, create, communicate! provides opportunities for visitors to explore the world of communications from the very early beginnings of coded messages to the latest state of the art technology.

Here children can learn how to communicate when stranded on a desert island, send signals from a yacht in distress, publish a newspaper, use a videophone or read the news in a television studio.

Things is a new exhibit gallery which encourages children to question and discover what things do, how and why they are made and how they affect our lives. The 'things' range from sample day-to-day practical objects to the latest technological equipment.

Here children can choose the right tool for the job, decide if something is real or fake, design a bike or change the features of a giant mechanical head by pressing buttons and operating levers.

There is also a special, discrete section for pre-school toddlers where they can play in a colourful environment which includes jungle creatures, a wooden bridge and a ruined temple.

It is expected that the lifespan of exhibits will vary from five to seven years and that the cost of devising, designing, fabricating and installing new exhibits in the future will need to be raised from various sources, including charitable foundations and corporate sponsorship. The first exhibit to be renewed was the Recycle area which was replaced by 'Things', a replica of the one that opened at the Science Museum in London in September 1995, and developed in conjunction with the Science Museum. Recycle had seemingly ceased to engage the enthusiasm and excitement of children, partly, it is thought, because recycling has become more generally accepted, especially within primary schools. The cost of developing new exhibits, from concept to operation, has been estimated at £1,000 per square metre.

Eureka! submitted a substantial millennium funding proposal (£9.5m) which will more than double the exhibition space of the children's museum and create a retail space development for lease to other traders. This is the start of the process of developing the whole of the 12.5 acre site and will refurbish and bring into use the original 1855 railway station as well as the Great Northern engine shed. The content and themes of the new exhibit area were at the time of writing being kept secret for reasons of commercial confidentiality. The local authority supported the millennium bid, which was successful.

Education and other activities

Over a quarter of Eureka's visitors are school groups. A typical visit will last for three hours: one hour focused on one of the seven sections in the museum; a second hour free to explore all over the museum; and a third hour for eating lunch, visiting the shop and enjoying the outside 'health trail' where children and adults can exercise and test their agility, balance and co-ordination. Teachers are provided with an education resource pack which includes detailed notes on how to get the best from each of the museum's sections and indicates links to the National Curriculum. There are also five special workshops which may be booked for school classes: understanding disability; making waves; video vibes; gears, levers and pulleys; dragons.

Free teachers' preview sessions are arranged to give teachers the chance to see Eureka! before they bring a group and to meet museum staff so that they can better prepare for their visit. Teachers' information days are also organised on specific topics within the context of 'Eureka! and the National Curriculum': in autumn 1995 two were being offered: 'making sense of information technology' and 'health education and primary children'.

During the year there is a variety of other activities: the 1995 programme listed a weekend of circle dancing; a library power week and an environment week; 'April magic' during the Easter holidays; 'Mechanical mayhem' each day spring through early summer; 'Treasure!' (stories and drama about pirates) during summer weekends and half-term and daily through the summer holidays; 'Space' (audiovisual exploration) during the autumn half-term and weekends and 'Big fibs and tall stories' during winter weekends and through the Christmas holidays. The museum also offers children's parties at Eureka!

Eureka! includes a cafeteria and a shop, selling souvenirs and educational toys. The cafeteria is franchised to an independent operator.

Eureka! is located below the railway station at the 'bottom end' of Halifax. It has its own very extensive car- and coach-parking facilities. Signage to Eureka! from the town and from the main roads leading into Halifax is both comprehensive and clear.

Facts and figures

Since its opening Eureka! has proved very popular and had welcomed its millionth visitor by November 1994. Its annual attendance is about 400,000, of which school groups comprise a quarter, a proportion which is increasing. Although 50% of the visitors come from Yorkshire and Humberside, only 4% are actually from Halifax itself. Its catchment area is basically the north of England, coast to coast, and from Tyneside to Leicestershire. Within that area it is possible to travel to and from Halifax within the day and spend three hours there. For schools the journey time must be no more than one and a half hours each way so that the visit can start and finish within the six hours of a typical school day.

The cost of visiting Eureka! (1997 prices) is £4.95 for persons over 12 years and £3.95 for children between three and 12. The under-threes are admitted free. There is a special rate of £3 per head for pre-booked school groups and other parties. Given the cost of transport in addition this can make the cost per pupil for a school group as much as £10, a not insignificant amount for many parents. As a consequence Eureka! reports a tendency for its visitors to be from better-off areas, and children from disadvantaged areas to be less likely to attend. There is presently no system of free or subsidised admissions to counter this trend.

Eureka! does not participate in the 'passport to leisure' scheme organised by the local authority, which has reciprocal arrangements with the neighbouring cities of Leeds and Bradford. The 'passport' scheme offers reduced price entry to persons who qualify as being unable to afford the commercial entrance costs, typically the unemployed, persons on benefit, etc, and they are issued with an ID card.

The operational budget is about £1.5m per annum and the museum earns 95% of that from its admissions and other sales. The remaining 5% has to be raised from charitable sources, primarily from the continuing support of the Vivien Duffield Foundation. However, the operational budget does not include provision for the renewal or refurbishment of exhibits, nor does Eureka! have any finance charges to pay, given the generosity of its original sponsor and the basis on which the museum site was made available by the local authority.

Organisation

Eureka! is structured as an educational charitable trust. Appointment to the board is by invitation and there is no provision for the local community (for as example represented by the local authority or by the local education department) to be involved as of right in the governance of the museum trust. An educational advisory group has, however, been established.

There are about 10 permanent full-time staff with up to 70 full-time equivalent others, depending on the season. A large number of the staff are young people, for example teacher-training or childcare students, making use of Eureka! to obtain experience which will be of direct value to them in their future careers. Staff on the floor who interact with visitors are described as 'enablers', their key role described in the original Children's Experience Centre proposal as: 'to help visiting children, answer questions, demonstrate exhibits, and suggest other lines of exploration. Given the wide range of visitors, the need for flexibility, skill and imagination on the part of the enabler will be stressed.'[8]

The palpable success of Eureka! is evidenced not only by the number of people who visit it but also by the array of awards it has received, ranging from the English Tourist Board's 'Visitor Attraction of the Year' (1993) to the British Tourist Authority's 'Yorkshire Loo of the Year' (1994); from the Royal Institute of British Architects' 'Main Architecture Award' (1993) to the Roy Castle Good Air Award (1994).

Some issues and trends

Eureka! has a unique position as the only acknowledged children's museum in Britain. It is therefore useful to try and draw some key points from the Eureka! story which should be considered by others considering a similar project elsewhere.

Competition: Eureka! has a regional role and is in competition with other major visitor attractions such as Alton Towers, vying with them to attract sufficient visitors to be sustainable. However, the experience in New England, for example, is that a large regional children's museum (Boston) can co-exist with as many as nine others within a two-hour drive. The question is: what type of other children's museum might co-exist with Eureka! within the north of England?

Regional role: Eureka! is in many ways a regional institution rather than a Halifax organisation. It serves the region and happens to be based in Halifax. One consequence of this, and of the way in which Eureka! came to the town in the first place, is that its community links are not well developed and there is neither the sense nor the fact of community ownership that are true of the majority of children's museums in the United States.

Economic impact: Because of its success Eureka! undoubtedly has a significant impact on Halifax. This is hard to quantify, but with over 90% of the visitors coming from outside the town it might be assumed that their spending would benefit shops, hotels, cafes and other local traders. Eureka! estimates its economic impact as having been worth £18m to the local economy over the first three years of operation.

However, local traders are not so sure. Their perception is that many visitors come to Eureka!, park in the museum's car parks but leave directly from Eureka! without visiting the rest of the town. They point to the extensive signage which helps visitors find Eureka! but which does not encourage the reverse flow into the town itself. It is feared that the proposed new retail development at Eureka! may exacerbate this phenomenon.

Educational resource: One of the most important, and apparently growing, roles of

Eureka! is to serve as a major educational resource for primary schools in the north of England. Teachers and pupils can access the sort of hands-on experiential inquiry facilities at Eureka! which no school, or local education authority, can support on its own. Increasingly these can be used to back up teaching of the National Curriculum. Supporting projects like Eureka! is one way in which the education world might in future strengthen the educational resource available to it. However, as education spending is withdrawn from the local authorities in favour of delegation to school budgets Eureka! has to market its service direct to the schools rather than seek financial support from the local education authorities.

One-off: Because Eureka! is the only one of its kind in Britain there is very much a sense that it is 'out on a limb' with only very few (partly) kindred organisations to associate with and to network with. This contrasts sharply with the situation in the United States with the extensive network of children's museums and their sense of being a 'movement'. It especially affects staffing as there is little career opportunity potential. The recent link between the Science Museum and Eureka! as regards the 'Things' exhibit shows the potential value of networking and sharing.

Affordability: The danger of Eureka! becoming essentially a middle-class service appears to be real. It is a problem which Eureka! cannot necessarily solve on its own, given that it must seek to pay its way financially. However, it has been suggested that joining the 'passport to leisure' scheme would permit people to attend Eureka! who otherwise are prevented by cost. This would increase rather than decrease income as those given reduced rate entrance would otherwise never have attended.

Given that organisations such as Eureka! have to be financially self-sufficient the ultimate solution may be to organise some form of subsidy – from the public sector, via a special trust, or through corporate sponsorships. Only thus can society ensure that potential visitors from disadvantaged areas are not prevented from accessing the Eureka! experience because of cost.

Viability: It seems clear that a project such as Eureka! is always likely to require some form of financial support to survive in the long-term. Ninety-five per cent self-sustaining on its basic operational costs, Eureka! is doing as well as the best in the United States and far better than the majority, where achieving 60% is a good average. The implications, however, are that projects need to be free of debt as regards the original capital (including obtaining the site/premises) and that finance for the refurbishment and renewal of exhibits has to be raised separately on a regular basis.

The wider scene in Britain

Many of the services offered and the techniques used by US children's museums are to be found in the work and practice of a variety of institutions and organisations in this country. Some British organisations have similar characteristics to children's museums and in the United States would be likely to consider themselves a form of children's museum. However, the local multifunctional institution, which is the archetypal US children's museum, is not to be found.

The following pages survey some of those organisations closest to children's museums. The British Interactive Group (BIG) (see Appendix two) lists some 45 institutions with hands-on interactive displays in its 1996 directory, including two mobile displays, and 15 designers and fabricators of interactive exhibits.

'Hands-on' in museums and galleries

Although they may have been pioneering in the 1960s when Michael Spock introduced the idea of 'hands-on' to the Children's Museum in Boston, interactivity and experiential exploration are now much more commonly accepted practice throughout the museum and galleries world. With the extraordinarily fast changes in computer-based technology it is now usual to find quite sophisticated computer-based 'interactives' to illustrate or amplify exhibits. There is an 'interactive continuum' which runs from pushing buttons and selecting choices at one end to the touching, smelling, feeling, doing style of exploration at the other.

Despite the trend towards interactivity, there are still museums and displays which are not even on the continuum, where glass cases full of exhibits to be looked at remain the order of the day. Among these are the Museums of Childhood in Edinburgh and Bethnal Green, London, which are quite different from the hands-on concept of a children's museum. While most of these 'glass case museums' do run educational programmes and organise special holiday-time events which are activity-based, the museum experience itself remains essentially static.

Nonetheless, 'Please touch' is generally more common in museums nowadays and, increasingly, is expected by visitors. The leaflet for Exeter's **Maritime Museum** proclaimed: 'Ours is a "please touch" museum' and described its 'touch and explore policy'.[9] The distinction between 'museum' and 'visitor attraction' becomes increasingly blurred as both compete for similar markets – for the general public, for the holidaymakers and tourists, and for school and other educational groups.

In the case of museums and art galleries, interactivity is usually linked to the educational services offered. The 'St Kilda Explored' exhibition at the **Kelvingrove Museum and Art Gallery** in Glasgow (October 1995 to August 1996) combined a reconstruction of St Kildan houses and a display of sound effects, diagrams, maps and photographs with a hands-on discovery room, where St Kildan artefacts could be studied at close quarters; some to be picked up, some to be observed under perspex. The discovery room also included written material for study purposes. For younger children there was a facilitated 'archaeological dig' where real artefacts could be uncovered from sand and pebbles, and a quiet drawing corner.

SEARCH is Hampshire County Council's hands-on centre where history and natural history items from the Council Museum's Service collections can be handled and studied with as few constraints as possible. SEARCH is aimed specifically at schools and an 'expert' interpreter/demonstrator is provided to work with each group. The **Jodrell Bank Science Centre** describes itself as 'the Science Centre where visitors can get physical with the Universe, energy and the environment through hands-on exhibits and fascinating displays',[10] while 'Science Raids' at the **University of York** is a project which aims to take science into the local community, mostly through 'short tailor-made hands-on weekends'.[11]

'Start' was an interactive art exhibition targeted at three to five year-olds by the **Walsall Museum and Art Gallery** which ran from May to July 1995. The planning and process of the initiative has been described in a special booklet ... *just like drawing in your dinner* ... published by the gallery.[12] The exhibition was designed to be attractive and interesting to young children and combined pictures displayed at child height with sculptures within reach, some of which could be touched. There were also hands-on activities: perspex masks, finger painting on a computer touch-screen, making fabric collage paintings and tissue collages, and sessions with artists in residence.

The **Ulster Museum** in Belfast offers a wide range of education services, including its Science Discovery Bus. One of the star attractions on the bus is 'Stuffee', the six foot high soft sculpture who originated from the Pittsburgh Children's Museum. Dr Sally Montgomery, head of education at the museum, describes how 'Stuffee, who receives most of the fan mail, is used in an unique health education lesson. Not only do children marvel at his seven metres of intestine but also giggle at his enormous sandwich as it emerges from his over-sized lunch box.'[13] The bus was launched in May 1990 to take 'the riches and resources of the museum to the economically and socially deprived areas in the city'. Dr Montgomery explains: 'With the new emphasis in the Northern Ireland curriculum on primary evidence, hands-on experience is essential, but individual schools cannot command the necessary resources.'

A further modest example of museum provision similar to that found in a children's museum is the Discovery Centre at the **Natural History Museum** in London. Here there is a 'please touch table' and a 'feely box', the chance to make 'flying seeds' and to work out 'how fishes float'. During Easter and summer holidays the Discovery Centre offers special events such as story-telling, model-making and art activities.

At London's Science Museum

The Science Museum, London has interactive sections targeted at children and young people and they are in quite striking contrast to the remainder of the museum which tends still to be based on the 'observe and look' tradition. The Science Museum has been one of the pioneers of interactivity in Britain.

Launch Pad is perhaps the best known, set up in 1986 as Britain's first permanent interactive display and described as:

'A hands-on gallery full of demonstrations, experiments and puzzles for visitors to try for themselves. The exhibits provide a setting where people of any age can explore the principles behind the technology we all use every day – in communications, building, transport and many other applications.'[14]

There are over 50 different exhibits and the focus is technology. Although aimed at (and enjoyed by!) all age-groups it tends to be most suitable for the 7 to 13 year-olds. It is a very popular visit for school groups and most of the 300,000 school child visits that are made to the museum each year will visit Launch Pad while they are there. Indeed the museum estimates that half of its total of 1.6 million visitors each year visits Launch Pad. 'Explainers' are on hand in the Launch Pad to help and daily science shows are performed on such topics as Structures, Light & Colour, Papermaking, Electricity & Magnetism. Although these shows are not specially arranged for school groups, many schools take advantage of them.

Flight Lab is a smaller hands-on section with 21 exhibits which tends to work better for the slightly older age-group of 10 to 16 years. It has demonstrations and experiments designed to show how aircraft are built, how they fly, how they are controlled and how their engines work. Specific exhibits include a hot air balloon, wind tunnels and computer simulations.

More recently opened in September 1995 is **On air**, an interactive radio station exhibit is aimed at teenagers and offering them the chance to produce a radio programme through teamwork.

In the basement, the **Things** gallery also opened in September 1995 and is aimed at children of primary school age. Things is about how things work – the history, science and technology of familiar and unfamiliar objects – and it is located alongside another exhibition called 'The secret life of the home' into which a number of interactive exhibits have also been incorporated.

The **Garden** is a gallery for children under six years where they can have a first introduction to science and technology with interactive sound and light displays, a water area and a construction area. A puppet theatre, role play and 'discovery bags' are also available.

Food for thought is about how science and technology have affected what we eat and how it is prepared. Although not aimed particularly at children, it includes a number of interactive exhibits and is popular with school groups. Explainers are on hand at all times and interactive demonstrations are given at intervals.

On busy days numbers have to be restricted in the hands-on galleries and special entrance tickets are issued, valid for time-limited visits. The museum organises sleep-over visits which include an educational evening programme.

The Science Discovery Centres

The major science discovery centres in Aberdeen, Bristol and Cardiff are perhaps closest, after Eureka!, to US children's museums like the Science Discovery Museum at Acton, Massachusetts. Inspired by the Exploratorium in San Francisco which opened in 1969 and now has over 600 interactive science exhibits, Satrosphere (Aberdeen), the Exploratory (Bristol) and Techniquest (Cardiff) all offer hands-on science exhibits, educational facilities for teachers and for school groups and fun and learning for visitors of all ages.

Satrosphere, describing itself as 'Scotland's first and only hands-on science centre', was founded in 1988 'to stimulate public awareness, especially in the north-east of

Scotland, of the significance of science and technology to society ... by providing an interactive exhibition for exploring scientific concepts and applications'.[15] An additional aim was to make Aberdeen and north-east Scotland more attractive to visitors.

Sponsored by Grampian Region, by Aberdeen City, by industry and by higher and further education, Satrosphere eventually opened the doors of its 7,000 square feet of exhibition space in 1990. About 80 exhibits of a total collection of over 160 are in use at any one time and the exhibition theme is changed four times each year. Satrosphere has its own workshops in which old exhibits are repaired and renovated and new ones designed and fabricated. Exhibits are also constructed under contract for other organisations. In July 1995 Satrosphere launched its 'Science on the move' programme of specially designed travelling exhibitions available 'to visit schools, community centres, shopping malls, railway stations – anywhere people, young and old, meet'.

Fifty thousand visitors go to Satrosphere each year of whom about 8,000 are with school parties. A mini multilingual guide has recently been published. The educational programme includes themed activities which relate to the science parts of the school curriculum and special science classes. Regular preview sessions are arranged for teachers to help them better prepare for visits, and in-service training sessions are attended by over 100 primary teachers each year. Holiday-time workshops for children are organised and in March 1996 Satrosphere published a walking trail around the city centre with stopping points for 18 different hands-on scientific activities: these include identifying seagulls, looking at the effects of wind-tunnelling and using lichens to estimate air pollution.

Satrosphere employs seven full-time and four part-time staff as well as 13 floor staff, known as 'redcoats'. Its annual budget of £0.25m is covered by admissions and sales (shop and café) (40%), private business sponsorship and trust income (26%) and local government grants (34%).

Bristol's **Exploratory** claims to derive from the inspiration of Francis Bacon who described in *The New Atlantis* (1627) an imaginary science centre called the House of Salomon, designed for both amusement and hands-on investigation of scientific phenomena.[16] The first hands-on science centre to open in Britain, the Exploratory ran a series of temporary exhibitions from 1984 and since September 1987 has been located in the fine old station building designed and built by Brunel in 1835 for the Great Western Railway.

The Exploratory has more than 150 exhibits or 'plores' as they are known in Bristol after the new 'word' they have introduced into the English language: 'plore; n; an object or experiment for investigation or discovery by hands-on or other active exploration.'[17] Its exhibit area covers some 15,000 square feet.

The Exploratory emphasises that 'scientific ideas are best understood by actually trying them out' and reinforces this not only through its hands-on 'plores' but also through suggested experiments which can be carried out in the home or at school.

> 'Our purpose is to help you explore science for yourself – in your own time, in your own home and in your own way. Science is not something you do only at school and at places like the Exploratory: it is very much part of your daily life',

writes Professor Richard Gregory, chairman of the trustees and founder of the Exploratory.[18] The Exploratory's 'plores' are organised into two broad-based themes: 'How do we experience the world?' and 'Why is the world the way it is?'

Educational programmes represent, as with Satrosphere, Techniquest and Eureka!, a significant part of the work of the Exploratory. Free preparatory visits are offered to teachers and special teachers' evenings arranged. Five standard visit programmes are offered, variously linked to Key Stages 1 to 4 in the National Curriculum. These include 'Explorer visits' (a general visit accompanied by the Exploratory's floor staff, known as 'pilots', who will help groups use and understand the exhibits) and more specialised visits: 'Star Dome Planetarium'; 'Science Workshops' (chemistry experiments); 'Pathways' (about bridges, colour, sound, movement, light, electricity); 'Stradivarium' (sound and music). Throughout the year there are special events at the Exploratory. In the summer of 1995 there was 'Megafun with computers', a computer playground with 22 interactive computer installations. During November 1995 'Fantastic fireworks!' was scheduled for the 4th to find out 'what makes bangers bang, catherine wheels colourful and rockets take off!' Later that month were scheduled a dramatic presentation about Marie Curie and 'game style' presentations about the development of early plastics, 'Parkesine' and 'Bakelite'.

The Exploratory is an independent, educational, registered charity. It is funded mainly through admission income, grants from foundations and corporate sponsorship. It receives 170,000 visitors each year of whom 35% are school parties. There are 16 full-time staff and 25 part-time.

In May 1996 Millennium Commission funding was announced for a new home for the Exploratory as part of a harbourside development in Bristol city centre. The new

Exploratory will eventually increase to 400 hands-on exhibits and will include a 150-seater planetarium and Virtual Theatre, laboratory spaces and an 'Explanatory'. The Explanatory will use the latest interactive computing technology to provide information about exhibits tailored to visitors' needs and interests.

Cardiff's **Techniquest** first opened its doors to the public in 1986 in shop-front premises in the city centre opposite Cardiff Castle. There were 35 hands-on exhibits which attracted 1,000 visitors each week. Within months the opportunity came, with help from the Development Corporation, to move to the Cardiff Bay development area. The size of the exhibition area doubled and so did visitor numbers. It was possible to introduce an education programme, linked to the National Curriculum.

By May 1995 Techniquest moved again, within the bay development area, into a purpose-built Science Discovery Centre, designed around the steel framework of a former dockside heavy engineering workshop. The new building of some 30,000 square feet has been backed by European funding, the Wales Tourist Board and the Welsh Development Agency.

Techniquest describes itself as a 'new style of centre' which 'is neither a museum nor a funfair, but contains elements of both'.[19] One hundred and sixty of its interactive exhibits are on view and in use at any one time 'suitable', it says, 'for all ages – from four to 94!' Most of the exhibits are designed and manufactured in-house.

There is also a 100-seat semicircular lecture theatre; a small planetarium; a 'discovery room' where the contents of 'curiosity boxes' are used to provide focused hands-on learning experiences for junior school groups; a library available to teachers and group leaders and also (by prior arrangement) to small groups of secondary school pupils; and the Lab where more structured projects and activities are organised.

Techniquest is very much an educational resource, heavily used by school groups. A programme of theme weeks relates to curriculum Key Stages for primary and secondary pupils. Visiting groups receive a lecture/demonstration in the theatre or planetarium and the visit is supported with written material for teachers. Other focused visits can be devised to concentrate on a particular subject.

Techniquest education kits have been developed to support the teaching of National Curriculum science in primary schools and are available for hire. They cover five themes: Energy; Forces and Structures; Light and Colour; Materials; Ourselves. Pre-visits by teachers are encouraged and teacher preview sessions are arranged for the different theme weeks. INSET courses focus on particular areas of the National

Curriculum. Techniquest has an education team to plan and deliver its range of educational activities as well as the duty floor staff helpers, known as 'the green team'. There is a travelling planetarium and various table-top exhibits which can be accessed by schools.

Other facilities at Techniquest include a café, a science shop and a packed lunch picnic area. All facilities are available for hire on '360' evenings in the year and during the day subject to availability.

Techniquest is a registered educational charity committed to the promotion of science, engineering and technology. Its turnover is about £12m per year of which 55% is earned from admissions, from the shop and café, from building exhibits for other centres and from consultancy. 250,000 visitors attend Techniquest each year with entrance fees ranging between £2.50 and £4.50. There are 17 full-time staff and up to 60 occasional assistants.

Around the country there are a number of smaller science discovery centres offering a service to local primary schools and to the visiting public. Two such are **Curioxity** in Oxford and **Discovery** in Weymouth.

Curioxity opened in 1990 with just 16 interactive exhibits. Its two main aims are:

*   To provide a central innovative educational resource for science and technology in Oxfordshire aimed particularly at primary teachers and children and their parents.

*   To promote a better public understanding of science and technology.[20]

Curioxity has also worked with older children and with adults, including having sixth-formers translate exhibit instructions into French and German for foreign visitors. It was set up by the Oxford Trust, a charitable organisation which aims to encourage the study and application of science and technology, with financial support from Apollo Leisure (UK) Ltd. During 1996 it was refurbished and reorganised.

Discovery is a privately owned centre offering 'Science Fun for Everyone'.[21] It has over 60 exhibits in its 2,200 square feet building in the Old Harbour area of Weymouth. Opened in 1992, it offers a service to school groups as well as to the public. A recent innovation has been the opening of a public access Internet terminal in the centre. Discovery is wholly dependent on its income from admissions.

Visitor attractions

We have seen earlier that the distinction between tourist attractions and museums is becoming blurred, in the sense of what they offer and how they offer it. This is the world of 'infotainment' and 'edutainment' where people have fun but also learn something. The past is brought to life, history and other cultures are re-enacted for us, we go underground into mines, or underwater to observe sea-life, we eat medieval banquets in costume in castles, we visit farms to watch and even join in the daily round of a 'real' farm.

Learning while having fun is reinforced through learning by touching and learning by doing. Tourist visitor centres increasingly cater for school parties and prepare education packs linked to the National Curriculum.

As an example, the **Flambard's Village Theme Park** just outside Helston in Cornwall promotes 'unrivalled study opportunities' in its 'Victorian Village', in its 'Britain in the Blitz' exhibition, in its 'Chemist's Shop Time Capsule' and in its 'Aero Park' collection. An education support pack 'in line with National Curriculum guidelines' is provided to all teachers on confirmation of a booking. Flambards also has Cornwall's Exploratorium, exhibiting a very small selection compared with those to be found in the larger science discovery centres, but here they sit alongside bumper boats, a giant adventure playground, human cannonball rides, entertainment by clowns, jugglers and buskers, the canyon river family log flume, cyclopter monorail, aero-golf – 'and much, much more!'

'Drusilla's' is a family-run private park and small zoo designed for families with young children which has been in existence for more than 70 years. Its aim is to provide fun with education: 'The Fun Finding Out Day Out'.[22] More than 30 hands-on activities are spread throughout the zoo, all 'of a low-tech, kid-powered design', and requiring physical as well as mental skills. The park also includes 'Playland', an acre of play equipment designed to encourage imaginative play.

The Benedictine monks at **Buckfast Abbey** run a hands-on learning centre which receives about 11,000 schoolchildren visitors each year. The exhibits in the centre cover the life and work of the monks and the building techniques and materials used when the monks built the abbey earlier this century. Even the **Girl Guides** have opened a Heritage Centre in London which traces the history of the Association and includes over 16 hands-on exhibits, including bridge building, signalling, simple electric circuits, sight and sound, weather and the emergency services.

photo: Eureka! The Museum for Children

'Watch your skeleton pedalling!'

The continuing growth of these commercial facilities and the more competitive approach of museums and art galleries to attracting visitors are important factors which must be considered when determining the potential for a children's museum and the role it might play in its locality.

City farms

The community-based city farms in Britain also have some characteristics which relate them to US-style children's museums.

Windmill Hill in Bristol, for example, is a two-hectare city farm just half a mile south of the city centre. In 1976 the land was a derelict inner-city plot. Now it is a thriving focus of community activity and social projects.

The city farm is a small working unit run on sustainable, organic principles, with a 40-acre 'offshoot' some 20 miles away in the Somerset Levels where cattle, sheep and pigs are reared. The city site includes productive community gardens, individual allotments, animal and poultry pens, conservation areas, compost heaps, craft and sports facilities, an adventure playground and indoor play facilities, complete with a soft 'rumpus room'. There is a café and a shop which sells wholefoods and the farm's own produce and its organically reared free-range meats.

The city farm provides clubs for toddlers, children and young people and a special programme for women. It arranges adult education classes and training placements, and receives a regular stream of educational visits from schools. Like the children's museums it offers a birthday party service. It specialises in community care services: for people with mental ill-health, for people with learning difficulties, for people with disabilities, for the frail elderly and for carers.

More than 50% of its annual income is now achieved from income-earning activities, including contracts for community care. Future plans include the acquisition of a derelict factory nearby for conversion into workspace to house the farm's own profit-making and job-creating businesses, thus bringing its goal of independent financial sustainability closer.

Over 40 people are employed at the farm and there are more than 100 'timetabled' volunteers, to say nothing of the army of casual workers who help out from time to time. More than 800 local people are paid-up members, many of these being family members who come and go throughout the weeks and months both helping on the farm and using its services and facilities.

The **Almond Valley Heritage Centre** describes itself as an 'innovative museum which preserves, demonstrates and explains many aspects of West Lothian's varied past'.[23] Set up originally in the 1970s by local volunteers who were determined to salvage and restore the ancient water-driven machinery, Livingston Mill became one of Scotland's first city farm projects, with a range of rare breeds on its 16 acres. With support from the Livingston New Town Development Corporation and substantial volunteer input over more than 20 years, the farm and mill buildings have been restored, the water-driven machinery is in working order again and a range of new facilities and attractions have been developed.

The farm is now established as an independent museum with charitable status with the object of preserving and interpreting the heritage of West Lothian. It is grant-supported by West Lothian Council and is a 'commended attraction' of the Scottish Tourist Board. It has a community membership, the 'Friends of Livingston Mill', of 360 (including many families) and a board of trustees which includes nominees of the Friends, of the local authority and the Scottish Museums Council. The centre has five full-time staff and takes on another five seasonally as required.

In addition to the city farm and the mill machinery, the Heritage Centre comprises a Shale Oil Museum (celebrating West Lothian's role as the home of James 'Paraffin' Young and the cradle of the world's oil industry); a display of historic farm machinery; a narrow-gauge railway line; outdoor play and picnic areas; the 'oil shale adventure zone' (where children can 'rampage' around the replica of an abandoned oil works); and the soft play 'farm' and pedal tractor course for the under-fives. Livingston Mill also has a cafeteria and offers, in children's museum fashion, a full birthday party service. There is a museum shop.

School groups are welcomed to the farm for visits which focus on aspects of the working city farm, on the oil shale museum or on the water-driven mill. Visits include both explanation and demonstration with as much hands-on activity as is possible, according to the particular topic. In 1995, 25,000 schoolchildren visited Livingston Mill, coming from a catchment area of one and a half hours' journey time. Visits last about two hours and there is a special 50p person entrance charge for schools that become affiliate members of the centre for a £10 annual fee.

Day by day there is always something happening at the centre: cows coming in to be milked; animals being fed and cleaned; trailer trips to the outlying fields; volunteer work of all types. Additionally special seasonal events are arranged: Easter Eggcitement; Farm crafts weekend; Vintage vehicle rally; Animal magic; Railway shuntabout; Spooky happenings; Santa at Mill Farm.

Experiential safety learning

Another set of initiatives in Britain which echo some aspects of the children's museum philosophy and practices are the experiential safety learning projects. Often known as 'Crucial Crew events', these projects are usually two- or three-week events organised during the summer term to teach children about day-to-day hazards and about basic safety procedures. The emphasis is always on experiential learning: through doing, through realistic interaction with adult specialists, through having fun.

The project in North Cunninghame on Scotland's Ayrshire coast is known as **'Clued-up Kids'** and takes the form of some 10 'sets' or 'scenarios', set up in the grounds of a special school by the emergency and safety services to give a realistic re-enactment of potential hazards so that children can learn how to react and what action to take.[24] The sets change from year to year according to availability but are likely to include most of the following:

- railway safety: a Scotrail level crossing, staffed by British Transport Police;
- electricity: a Scottish Power sub-station, pole and lines, staffed by Scottish Power engineers;
- accident: ambulance service dealing with an injured person following a motor accident, staffed by a paramedic;
- water safety: body in a fire plus discarded flares, staffed by HM Coastguards;
- stranger danger: staffed by the police with volunteer actors;
- bag-snatch: staffed by the police and volunteer actors;
- road safety: vehicle braking test equipment, staffed by the Road Safety Officer;
- Hazard House: dangers in the home, staffed by Consumer and Trading Standards;
- fire: smoke-filled room in Hazard House, staffed by the fire brigade;
- public telephones: some working and some vandalised to be used to report various incidents;
- drugs awareness: staffed by Drugs Project outreach workers.

photo: Science and Society Picture Library

*The Launch Pad at London's Science
Museum was set up in 1986 as Britain's
first permanent interactive display and is
described as 'A hands-on gallery full of
demonstrations, experiments and puzzles'.*

The emphasis is on realism and on appropriate action in response to each hazard encountered. Learning is reinforced through a debriefing and follow-up work back in the classroom.

Clued-up Kids is targeted at primary six children, and in 1995 1,500 children attended the event from 35 schools during a three-week period in June. Events such as Clued-up Kids are funded usually through the local authority, through business sponsorship and by the commitment of time and energy from the participating services and organisations.[25]

Hazard Alley is a full-time permanent 'interactive indoor educational safety centre' in Milton Keynes.[26] It is the only one of its kind in Britain and is run by a charitable company, The Safety Centre (MK) Ltd. Hazard Alley is located on an industrial estate within a 10,000 square feet factory unit. The centre is entirely indoors.

There are 12 scenarios: hazard house kitchen (with fire); hazard house lounge (including the after-effects of a burglary); garden; building site; road safety; railway; petrol filling station; a dark alley (personal safety); farmyard; playground; water danger; electricity. There is also a changing seasonal display provided by Consumer and Trading Standards (eg: dangers of fireworks in the autumn).

Hazard Alley is open all weekdays and will also take evening bookings and make special arrangements for the weekends if requested. It is aimed at seven to 12 year-olds and most bookings come from primary schools and from youth groups such as Cubs, Brownies and church groups. Some 12,000 children visited the centre during its first year of operation for an entrance fee of £2.50 each. Groups travel from as far as a 90-minute journey in each direction.

Preparatory and back-up material is provided to teachers on confirmation of a booking and this is fully linked to the National Curriculum. All visitors receive a certificate and a pack of safety leaflets on completion of their visit.

A maximum of 72 children can be catered for at any one time, visiting the scenarios in groups of six. Each group is taken around by a trained volunteer staff member who explains each scenario, engages the children in discussion and identifies both the hazards and the ways of dealing with them. There are four full-time and two part-time staff, two of whom are secondees: one from business and one from the fire service.

Hazard Alley earns about 25% of its income from admissions, from shop sales and from rentals of its small conference/seminar facility. The remainder of its income comes mainly from private sector sponsorship.

Being a permanent facility using volunteer staff on the floor inevitably means that Hazard Alley cannot be as realistic and experiential as, say, Clued-up Kids where children encounter seemingly real situations and definitely real police officers, firemen, coastguards and so on. Nevertheless the Safety Centre emphasises interaction and learning through the imaginative experience of everyday potentially hazardous situations.

Current initiatives in London

Attempts to create a children's museum for London have continued. The **Discovery Factory** is a charitable company set up in 1992 which has been working since then to establish a children's museum in the capital. In 1993 it commissioned a report from Lord Cultural Resources and Management to specify the site and space criteria, and staffing and training needs. A business plan was prepared. During 1994 and 1995 the Discovery Factory came close to securing premises in North Kensington, with financial support from the Council, from charitable trusts and through City Challenge. Unfortunately that scheme failed on planning permission, in particular with regard to traffic flow and the difficulties of car parking.

The Discovery Factory describes its intentions as:

> 'to reach children in the 2-12 age range. We intend to be wary of hi-tech gadgetry which sometimes results in children using interactive facilities like amusement arcades, though obviously technology will be used and its practical applications demonstrated. Children love also to dress up, to play shops, to step back in time and to find out for themselves such things as what their great grandparents wore, or even what it is like to be confined to a wheelchair. Exhibits will be designed with reference to the National Curriculum, in consultation with teachers and educationalists. Concepts such as communication, from hieroglyphics to printing presses to fax machines, will be literally explored by children. Younger children will be able to climb on a fire engine and experiment with a giant bubble machine.'[27]

Another proposal for a children's museum in London was developed during the summer of 1996 under the auspices of Stratford Development Partnership Ltd and with support from the Gulbenkian Foundation. Known as **Site C: a New Kind of**

Future for the Next Generation, the aim was to create a children's museum, located in the East End, with three main exhibit themes:

- 'Children like us': an exploration of how the lives of children all around the world have developed over the past millennium up to the present day with a spyhole into some children's lives today using satellite link-ups;

- 'Me and My Life': looking at the future world of work and leisure including what jobs will be available in the next millennium for children today and what skills they will need;

- 'Making decisions': experiencing how decisions are made, what the impact of this is on the environment – interactive facilities showing how different decisions lead to different effects.[28]

Other important features of the proposal included the close involvement of children in the planning and operation of the museum programmes (starting with the choice of name) and the establishment of a Children's Forum to work with the initial steering group during the design and development phase to ensure that their ideas and needs were incorporated. Also, volunteering schemes were planned to involve young people in the running of the children's museum and to enable local people to maintain a close involvement.[29]

The project further sought to 'redress the west London bias of London's museums and cultural facilities' by creating a significant museum in the east, in Stratford's emerging cultural quarter adjacent to a new multiplex cinema, the refurbished Theatre Royal and the Community Arts Centre.

Site C failed in its Millennium bid but its committee has continued to develop plans and appointed a part-time development officer in September 1997. The project is now known as the Stratford Children's Discovery Centre and has acquired a disused building for development as a children's museum.

CHAPTER FOUR

A glance across
The Channel —
and beyond

Et tous les ballons descendirent vers Pascal, dansèrent autour de lui, emmelèrent leurs ficelles et l'enleverent dans le ciel. Et Pascal commença un immense voyage autour de la terre.[1]

On Monday when the sun is hot
I wonder to myself a lot:
'Now is it true, or is it not,
'That what is which and which is what?'[2]

Children's museums are fast becoming a world-wide phenomenon. In 1996 the Association of Youth Museums listed people or organisations from 23 countries as AYM members or as delegates to the Interactivity Conference 1996. The world-wide database built up by the European Network (see Appendix three) has identified 13 children's museums in Asia (of which six are in India), five in Latin America, 16 in Central and North America outside the United States, one each in Australia and New Zealand and some 65 in Europe. While the numbers must be treated with caution, both because there is as yet no really comprehensive means of gathering data and because definitions vary about what is and what is not a children's museum, they do confirm a growing interest in the concept and the practice of children's museums around the world.

The interest is not all recent. The Lucknow Children's Museum in India, for example, opened in 1957 with its 16 galleries and basic aim of promoting the values of 'tolerance, hospitality, goodwill for all' and 'exposing the basic unity of mankind'.[3]

For some the US model has been the stimulus. In the Philippines:

'It was initially a dream of a mother who took her own kids to the Boston Children's Museum, then situated in an old house. The old house was transported to an old building in Manila, now come alive as the Museo Pambata!'.[4]

Elsewhere children's museums have evolved from or within existing museum institutions and that is held more generally to be the case in Europe where only 20% of children's museums are thought to be in the 'US style': that is independent, dealing with various subjects and themes, with a multiplicity of exhibits, and large in scale or with the capacity and the intention to grow.[5]

From the 1970s there have been examples of European museums creating special areas or exhibitions for children but, the European Network's research points out, 'these children's museums had to fit into an existing museum ... (they) were created according to the philosophy of the main museum they are part of. They also treat the subject of this main museum'.

The fieldwork for this chapter was based on visits to Amsterdam and Rotterdam in The Netherlands and to Berlin in Germany. Seven children's museums were visited, of which three have developed within the educational service of major ethnological museums, two having had a discrete identity as a children's museum for more than two decades, and one other is part of a local district museum. Of the three 'independents' two are akin to the US model, in particular the most recently opened children's museum, in Berlin, and one is a producer of short-term exhibitions, usually in close association with the city museum education service.

The Kindermuseum, Amsterdam

The children's museum at the Tropenmuseum in Amsterdam could not be more different from a typical US style children's museum. It was founded in 1975 within the educational service of the Royal Tropical Institute. Its method is to run one exhibition at a time of roughly two years' duration. Only children between the ages of six and 12 are admitted to the very structured programmes, adults being admitted for 10 minutes at the end of each programme to be shown around by the children! There is no casual public access, only participation in the group programmes.

A recent exhibition, 'Stories of where to go' finished at the end of August 1997 having run since April 1995. It presented the lifestyle of a clan of Aboriginal people from North Arnhem Land in Australia's Northern Territory and sought to introduce the children of Amsterdam to a quite different culture: semi-nomadic, with an oral rather than a written tradition, with little concept of property, with quite different relations to the land, the past, ancestors and spirits. Meticulously researched, and with full co-operation from the Aboriginal clan, the exhibition created a series of sets or scenarios depicting the landscape, the seasons, the culture and daily life. The programme introduced children to the stories (songlines), the traditions, singing, dancing, making music, painting – and what lies behind these activities, their significance.

The purpose behind the exhibition was to help children accept and absorb other cultures and traditions, rather than just learn about them: 'The Aborigines exhibition presupposes a multicultural society, and the naturalness and added-value of mixed cultures' ... 'As far as we know, not a single Aboriginal child lives in The Netherlands. It is not despite this fact, but because of it, that the topic on Aboriginal life has been chosen. In view of this subject, all persons are equal'.[6] The social background against which the theme was chosen is the growing multiculturality of Amsterdam: more than half of primary school children are of non-Dutch origin. Through the exhibition the children's museum was seeking to help Dutch and immigrant children integrate and become prepared for their society of the future.

The main target audience is primary school classes for whom special programmes are designed: of two and a quarter hours duration for 10 to 12 year-olds and of one and three quarters hour for six to nine year-olds. School classes come on all school days, while on Wednesday, Saturday and Sunday afternoons and during the holidays programmes are offered to the public, three each day of one and a half hours duration and at set times. Visitors may attend only at these times, and it is wise to book in advance.

School teachers are expected to undertake some 10 hours of preparation work with their class before the visit, based on a teachers' pack supplied by the museum, including a video for the older pupils and a music cassette. In this way children already know some of the stories and the music and can therefore more readily join in the activities. Many classes develop class projects around their visit, often in the case of the Aboriginal exhibition, making a pole of friendship to add to the museum's collection of such poles.

A programme takes the form of a dramatic story-telling and presentation by the museum's team of professional actors, singers, dancers, storytellers and explainers which evoke aspects of the Aboriginal way of life, traditions, customs and history. The group of children then subdivides into smaller groups, each with a member of museum staff, and has the opportunity to explore the exhibition and to become involved in a particular activity. Although it is the children 'who bring the exhibition to life' it is the 'staff members of the children's museum (who) are always present as intermediaries between the collection, the exhibition and the visitors'.[7]

Objects are for touching and using. The aim is not to make a collection attractive to children but to make the objects 'fit the story'. The research and development for a new exhibition starts almost as soon as the current one has opened. The next exhibition, about people from the Bolivian Highlands, opened in December 1997. This current exhibition has been in preparation since early 1996. It is the ambition of the

School programmes for Enchanted Worlds[8]

Enchanted Worlds: Daan's Coat (for the 4 and 5 year-olds)

In Enchanted Worlds children meet Mrs de Wit. She wants to show them The Square where she lives, and above all, The Well-loved Things Museum. It's still closed, but the director Daan Dingemans lives next door. Daan is so unhappy, for he has lost the key he always keeps in his coat. He's been looking for it everywhere. Mrs de Wit and the children decide to help him. Will they find the key ... ?

In this programme the children are dragged into solving some problems. They learn that you can exchange things with each other, but you always keep your well-loved things. In the end all turns out well and with a song the children say good-bye to Daan and Mrs de Wit. The teacher is asked to practise the singing of the song at school before their visit.

Enchanted Worlds: Party on the Square! (for the 7 to 9 year-olds)

The children are invited on The Square to celebrate the coming home of Mrs Bernadette Arnhem who has made a trip around the world. Together with the neighbours they decorate The Square. But it takes so long before she arrives! Everyone gets worried and they decide to go and look for her. They travel around the world and discover lots about all kinds of feasts. But will they find Mrs Arnhem, will there be a party ... ?

In this programme the children work together in small groups, with some tasks about different themes like clothes, music and food. They learn that their themes are parts of a successful party. The teacher is asked to make drawings with the children and to practise the singing of the song at school before their visit.

Enchanted Worlds: Dingemans is my name (for the 11 and 12 year-olds)

Some weeks before the visit the teacher receives a videotape and brief instructions to prepare the children for their visit to the museum. The videofilm explains what is meant by well-loved things. The children are invited to bring a well-loved thing of their own to school. They are asked to choose the three most attractive, special or strange objects and to take these along with them to the museum.

The children meet the people who live on The Square and they get involved in a scene through the objects they have brought with them. The director of the Well-loved Things Museum shows his collection. One chest, marked 'Things we know nothing about' opens up the worlds behind the objects. With a number of objects in a rucksack and with a ticket the children travel around the world in small groups, in order to find out the significance and inherent value of these objects. At the end of the trip each group has to choose one object to take back to The Square in Rotterdam. They return to The Square and the following scene is based on the children's experiences during their travel.

Highlights from the visit of each group are recorded on a videotape the group can keep. At school the children can watch the videotape which also gives some suggestions for the children and the teacher to talk over their experiences during their travels.

museum's director that a primary school child has the chance to see at least two different exhibitions at the museum in the course of a primary school career. Over 20% of Amsterdam primary schools visited the Aboriginal exhibition during its run and a total of 80,000 visitors was received.

Enchanted Worlds, Rotterdam

Het Reispaleis ('Enchanted Worlds') is the permanent children's exhibition run by the Education Service of the Volkenkunde Museum in Rotterdam (they eschew the designation 'children's museum' on the grounds that they run only one exhibition at a time). This relatively recent exhibition, for which planning started in 1993 and which fully opened in April 1995, also takes as its starting point the increasingly multicultural society in the city where more than half of schoolchildren have parents or grandparents who were not born in The Netherlands. The purpose of Enchanted Worlds is to 'help children form a positive, balanced view of their own culture and that of others'.[9]

Unlike the Amsterdam approach which depicts a culture not present in The Netherlands, Enchanted Worlds presents some of the different cultures which now make up so much of Dutch society, using everyday objects as a guide to the 'stories which lie behind them' – to the lives and feelings of the people to whom the objects belong and for whom they are important and to understanding the common feelings of humanity that transcend cultural differences.

*TV and Magnetic Interactive, Launch Pad, The Science
Museum, London.*

Enchanted Worlds consists of three scenarios. First, a Rotterdam square with a range of multicultural shops, offices and activities brought to life by actors; second, the Museum of Well-loved Things full of chests, each with objects that tell a special story, and one surprise chest of 'Things We Know Nothing About' which leads to; third, 'The World Behind the Objects', four separate areas allowing visitors to travel in The Netherlands, the lands of Islam (Turkey and Morocco), the Caribbean (Surinam) or Indonesia. Armed with a travel pass, children can research the stories behind specific objects as revealed through the appropriately furnished rooms filled with things to look at, to touch, to try out; videos to watch and interactive programmes to explore.

Enchanted Worlds offers special school programmes (see panel on page 94) for different age-groups. Each programme uses actors/explainers to bring the scenario to life and to engage the children in the message and in the exploration. Teachers are given information to help them prepare their classes for the visit.

Outside school hours Enchanted Worlds is open to the public and it is also possible to book for birthday parties at which 'the party guide takes the children on a (mystery) puzzle tour to find the birthday present, because the postman has mixed up all the mail!'[10]

Enchanted Worlds receives about 40,000 visitors each year and the exhibition is planned to run until August 1998 before being replaced.

Juniormuseum, Berlin

The Juniormuseum is to be found in the basement of Berlin's Museum für Völkerkunde and consists of two rooms and a corridor which lead off a large open area at the foot of the staircase, furnished with two huge glass cases and with tables and chairs ready for a group meeting. The Juniormuseum started in 1970, initially with small cases of objects taken from the main museum collections for children to look at.

Now the Juniormuseum mounts one exhibition each year, using objects from its parent museum's collection and selecting themes which introduce children both to the daily life of other cultures and to the idea of visiting and using museums. The emphasis is on touching and using, drama and doing, although there is still a place for objects to be observed behind glass.

The most recent exhibition ended in August 1997 and was about masks, their role and use in different cultures (including our own) and the different materials used to make them. In preparation is an exhibition about water – for bathing and for swimming. This is being developed in association with the museum's East Asian Department and will feature a Japanese water garden as well as European objects and practices.

Although the Juniormuseum is open to the visiting public for a limited time each week it is primarily targeted at primary-age children (8 to 12 years) and receives one class on four mornings each week. These opportunities are very quickly fully booked by schools that use the museum regularly year on year. Special arrangements can be made to receive a group in the afternoon. School visits last for between two and a half and three hours.

A typical school visit programme starts with an introduction to the theme of the exhibition for the whole class which is then divided into two groups. Each is taken on an explained tour of the exhibition to be looked at in the glass cases and on the walls of the corridor en route to the museum rooms. In one they will take part in a hands-on role play. During the masks exhibition this was a Zambian village in which the children learned about African village life, sang and danced, made music, made head-dresses, dressed up, wore masks – the whole culminating in a village festival. Meanwhile in the other museum room was the opportunity to experiment with making masks, something to take home.

Jugendmuseum, Schöneberg, Berlin.

A grand historic Berlin town house in Hauptstrasse with eight foot-high sunflowers in the garden is home to the Schöneberg District Youth Museum. It forms a part of the local council museum, one of 23 local museums throughout Berlin, although Schöneberg is the only district to have established a youth museum.

Although Schöneberg museum had received visits from schools for many years as part of its local educational programme, it was the racially motivated violence of the early 1990s which stimulated the present emphasis on working with young people. What could a museum do to promote harmonious living in the community, tolerance, respect for others; to help people understand the present through the past?

In 1994 the museum acquired its present building, which was surplus to municipal requirements following the reunification of East and West Berlin, for youth work purposes, and developed a two-pronged strategy: project work and a permanent exhibition serving school groups and the public.

The 8 May 1995 marked the 50th anniversary of the end of the war. The Youth Museum used it as the starting point for a major project involving classes from six primary schools and three secondary schools. For six months pupils and teachers, working with museum staff, researched different aspects of the end of the war and after the war: everyday life in 1945; the former Jewish synagogue and community in Schöneberg; the Bunker: its use in the war and since; reflections on the war and the ensuing half-century. Pupils interviewed members of their families and of the public, filmed and photographed, researched in the archives and at home, gathered objects, wrote material, made models, developed an exhibition – including a specially written piece of rap music to mark the opening – which was mounted in the Youth Museum from November 1995 until the following March. At the exhibition the young people who had created it were the experts.

The museum building itself had been renovated during 1995 by young people on a training programme (by young people for young people) and the current exhibition, 'Wunderkammern – Wunderkisten in den Gelben Räumen und im Keller' (Amazing Cabinets and Chests in the Yellow Rooms and in the Cellar), opened in May 1997 and is due to run until the year 2002.

The bright yellow rooms on the ground floor contain an intriguing layout of 54 numbered chests (2 x 1 x 0.5 metre) each containing a selection of themed objects; some precious and rare, some unusual, some everyday, ordinary articles; some relating to the distant past, some to the past of living memory, some to the present; some dealing with historical or political issues, some dealing with social or more sensitive issues; some dealing with life as it was, some with life as it is today; some with the multiculturality of Berlin. Within the boxes is a wealth of fascinating detail and some textual information – the stimulus to further exploration which is carried out in the cellar. Here are other yellow boxes with relevant objects to be touched and tried, clothes to dress up in, reference material in card index format to examine. Elsewhere there is the white room: the workshop equipped with tools and materials for painting and for making models, for developing exhibition displays.

A school class visit is for four hours and starts with a dramatic introduction when the group is 'transported' to the year 2097 and meets a woman from that future era who is having problems making sense of a box of ordinary objects from 1997. The children help her understand. Then they have time to explore the 54 yellow chests freely before dividing into four small groups, each with a member of the museum staff, and selecting their own topic for research and exploration. They use the appropriate box from the cellar, using the reference material, looking again at the yellow chest exhibition and prepare some form of project report, display, picture or model.

The Youth Museum's target age is eight to 14 years although it will work with both younger and older children, even as old as 18 to 20 year-olds. It encourages older children to retain their association with the museum and currently employs six young people as explainers when the museum is open to the public on Wednesday, Thursday and Sunday afternoons.

Kinder und JugendMuseum im Prenzlauer Berg, Berlin

The KJM is a project of an independent organisation, Netzwerk Spiel/Kultur, which was formed after the Berlin wall came down by people and organisations whose roots had been in former East Germany. Other Netzwerk projects include a playground, a media workshop and a children's rights campaign to have the voting age lowered.

The KJM started as a museum without walls, taking projects out into the community in its 'museum suitcases'; a community-based starting point similar to many small US children's museums.

> 'The specialty of the museum suitcase lies in its flexibility and its simplicity. It can be used just as well in the school as in a museum. The suitcase is always "unpacked" by a museum worker and the school children are actively involved in the exploration and are encouraged to handle the objects from the suitcase. A suitcase session requires at least two hours, with the chance for more intensive working in small groups'.[11]

Now KJM has a shop front exhibition area (opened in September 1996) with three offices, workshop, storage rooms to the rear (since 1994) on the ground floor of a tenement block in a suburban street. The current exhibition, designed and developed by KJM, is based on the theme of mirrors and was partly financed by the children's museum in Munich to which the exhibition will go after its four-month spell in Berlin. KJM aims to change the theme of its main exhibition two or three times each year. The museum receives regular school class visits and is open to the public (20 being the maximum at any one time) on four afternoons each week.

However, exhibits such as 'Mirrors' are relatively new to KJM whose reputation has been built up working on local history projects with school classes who dedicate one

Barrel organs from Prenzlauer Berg: mission statement[12]

Just a few streets away from our museum an old sign still indicates the location of the factory of the Italian Giovanni Battista Bacigalupo where he produced Germany's most famous barrel organs. The company existed for more than 80 years until its closure in 1975.

We had found an exciting subject to carry out researches into the history of craftmanship and culture in our neighbourhood. We thought that the barrel-organ could be a wonderful way of combining the past and the present. Elderly people would be reminded of their own childhood and children might become curious about past times by listening to this no longer used musical instrument. Consequently our project sponsored by the Foundation for Youth and Family Berlin was called 'Childhood in Prenzlauer Berg – in the past and today'.

One hundred years ago the barrel-organ was popular for street music and as an everyday entertainment for the people. Now we walked through the streets and the backyards of Prenzlauer Berg like the barrel-organ players at the turn of the century together with children and a borrowed original Bacigalupo organ. What we had hoped and expected happened: children gathered around the barrel-organ, and old inhabitants of the neighbourhood came by and told stories of their childhood when barrel-organ players moved around regularly.

Being occupied more and more with the Bacigalupo company we realised that there was more to come out of this subject than only the fascination of the barrel-organ as an instrument. The Italian immigrant family Bacigalupo, of which have lived three generations in Prenzlauer Berg since 1873, is a good example of the living and working conditions of immigrants in Germany at the time of the Kaiserreich to the time of the German Democratic Republic. Looking at the example of the Bacigalupo family it becomes especially clear how immigrants always have influenced culture and society. Though Berlin was famous for its barrel-organs and you could sometimes see one of them in its streets, there are not many people who know of the Italian influence on production and distribution of these instruments. That was one reason why we decided on 'Italian immigration to Prenzlauer Berg' as the main theme for our project.

We also had pedagogical reasons to put emphasis on the subject of immigration. Because of the lack of contacts with foreigners in the more isolated GDR, there are still feelings of resentment against members of ethnic communities among the population in the districts of former East Berlin, including Prenzlauer Berg. The low percentage of about 3% of immigrants in East Berlin indicates the still strong reservations against foreigners. It is well known that many foreigners don't want to live in the eastern part of the city and that indeed there has been violence against Turkish youth. We see an important responsibility of the Kinder und Jugendmuseum by bringing different cultures together and so inspire some cultural learning. By the example of the Bacigalupo family local children can experience why people had/have to leave their home country and settle in foreign countries. They can also learn how people are able to build up a new existence with creativity, imagination and perseverance despite a difficult starting point.

full week to working on a project. It all started with the Soap Shop – a fully equipped local soap making and retailing business which, like many others, was unable to compete in the reunified economy in the years after 1989. The elderly couple who had owned and run the shop donated it to KJM and it became the basis for a school project delving into the history of the Soap Shop, exploring the implications of reunification to small businesses, looking at the history of soap manufacture and retailing, looking at the local network of shops, testing out the ironing service which had been provided by the shop. The resulting exhibition took place in the local district museum where the children were the expert guides and explainers for the visiting public, including offering a free ironing service using the ancient machinery! After the exhibition the main shop furniture and equipment was relocated in the back room at KJM where it is still used by visiting school groups.

Subsequent project weeks have focused on a variety of local history themes, including a disused lead type printing press (now housed in the basement of a local school), the 125th anniversary of a local brewery (KJM brewed beer proved undrinkable!), the role and reminiscences of the child soldiers (Flakhelfer) of 1943, the history of the Berlin barrel organ and the local Italian factory that made them (see panel on page 101). The next project week will look at local archaeology.

The MuseoMobil (a 1960 former fire service lorry) takes KJM out into the community and also serves, when parked outside the shop, as an extra room for visiting school pupils. One ongoing project of the moment is the Internet international cookbook (visit at http://www.b.shuttle.de/museum). Another is the weekend flea-market, only for stallholders under the age of 16. The KJM also negotiates and organises hands-on visits 'behind the scenes' for parties of schoolchildren to other museums in Berlin.

KJM emphasises the role that children should play in deciding and organising the work of the museum; and its focus on the real events and experiences of everyday life: 'a museum run by children, with children, for children and youth together with adults'.[13]

Neues Universum, Berlin

Neues Universum (New Universe) is a small independent organisation which has been seeking to establish a permanent US style children's museum in Berlin for some 10 years. That remains their ambition, but for the moment a suitable location and the necessary funding package continue to elude them. While pursuing their main ambition Neues Universum had run over the years a number of short-term workshops and projects but in 1994 they applied their interest and their diverse expertise to developing high-quality, short-term exhibitions in association with the City of Berlin Museum Educational Service. The first of these, 'Der Fliegende Koffer' (the Flying Suitcase), ran for six weeks in 1995 at Berlin's Haus der Kulturen der Welt, during which time some 30,000 children visited.

The Flying Suitcase, funded by a grant from the German lottery, was about life in Ghana, featuring its landscape, history, people, customs and way of life. Its rationale was to promote humanity and tolerance 'so essential for the future of mankind and which can only grow through mutual learning and understanding amongst peoples'.[14]

The exhibition included a marketplace with shops and stalls, an area for making toys from scrap metal, a drumming workshop, necklace-making, building and painting a house in the African manner, hair-dressing, dressing up, a darkened 'rain forest' room with uneven floor and the smells and sound of the forest and even a real 'mammy wagon' to climb all over. All was hands-on activity (including attempting to carry full water pots on the head) led by exhibition staff drawn from the Ghanaian community living in Berlin.

In addition to the hands-on exhibition there were also glass cases of objects borrowed from the Museum für Völkerkunde. School visits (all booked out well in advance) lasted for one and a half hours, starting with a brief introduction after which the children were free to go to whichever activity stations interested them. Outside

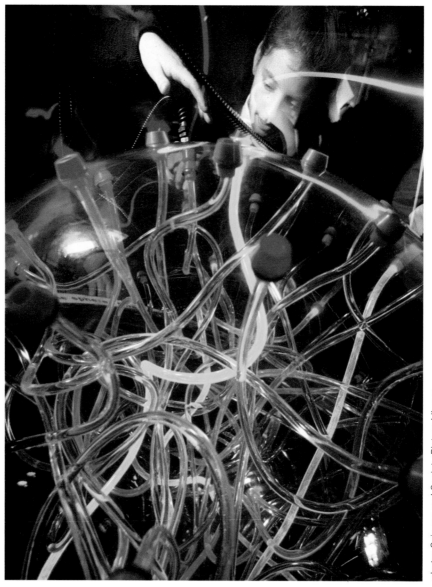

photo: Science and Society Picture Library

Discovering that light will follow a curve
in Light Pipes Interactive at The Science
Museum, London.

school hours the exhibition was open to the public. After Berlin the Flying Suitcase went on to children's museums in Duisburg and Vienna.

In April 1997 Neues Universum's second exhibition, 'Schall und Rauch' opened, again for six weeks at the Haus der Kulturen der Welt, again financed by the Lottery, again in association with the Museum Education Service and again to go on to Vienna. Schall und Rauch is about hearing and listening, about sounds and noise. One of the centrepiece exhibits was a giant climb-through ear.

In August 1997 Neues Universum organised a building site for children within the Potsdamer Platz area of the city, known as the biggest (re)building site in Europe. For four weeks children could attend the site, which was staffed by architecture students, use real building materials and tools (not child-sized ones) and explore a simple computer-aided design programme. The site was sponsored by all the building firms working at Potsdamer Platz and received 20,000 visitors, including many local building site workers bringing their own children.

Labyrinth, Wedding, Berlin

Labyrinth opened its doors as Berlin's newest children's museum on 13 September 1997, its first main exhibition, 'Bubbles', rented from the children's museum in Vienna. When it is fully functional, Labyrinth will be closest to the US style multifunctional children's museum. It will consist of one major exhibition hall, the contents of which will change twice a year. Already work is in hand on Im Labyrinth der Sinne' (In the Labyrinth of the Senses) to replace Bubbles in December 1997. 'Im Labyrinth der Sinne will take the form of a maze in which visitors will become aware – in a multitude of ways – of their five senses. It is planned that this exhibit will be available for hire or sale to other museums afterwards.

In addition to the main exhibition hall, Labyrinth will include a reading room for children, containing material which relates to the theme of the main exhibition and located next to the parents' café which will serve both as a meeting and waiting place for parents and as a parents' resource centre giving information and advice. A local history room will be developed (first theme: street games of the past), a media workshop, a quiet room, music room and a toddler space. Labyrinth will also include a museum shop and a café, the latter franchised out to a local non-profit organisation which employs people with disabilities.

The borough of Wedding is one of former West Berlin's more disadvantaged areas and has a high percentage of Turkish immigrants in its population. A motivating purpose of Labyrinth is to reach out to the disadvantaged and to the immigrants, to provide a museum in the suburb rather than in the city centre, to enrich the cultural opportunities for local children and their parents, to replace the lost freedom to play and explore in the streets and the neighbourhoods.

Labyrinth has been established within a wider project, Fabrik Osloer Strasse, which is a collection of local social and economic projects gathered together in one extensive set of buildings, a sort of social and economic workspace. Fabrik Osloer Strasse is home to training projects for young people (metal work and insulation), workshops for small businesses, a hostel for young people and for exchange groups, family projects in health awareness, baby and childcare, pre- and after-school childcare, youth groups and adult training, especially for women. Labyrinth's own part of the building is the listed turn-of-the-century machine-tool factory, with a striking brick façade giving onto the street.

In its prospectus Labyrinth emphasises its intention both to involve children in the planning and activities of the museum and its family orientation – the museum is for children and adults visiting, playing, exploring and learning together.

Key points and contrasts

These pages are no more than 'snapshots' of some European children's museum experience and practice. It is to be expected that the European experience will be varied in comparison to the US model given the diversity of history, culture and language throughout the continent. However from the snapshots and from the research and documentation of the European Network it is possible to draw out some key points and to identify some important contrasts.

To date in Europe it appears more likely that an institution considering itself a children's museum will have evolved within or from an existing museum, probably as part of the museum education service – and that it will exemplify a trend to introduce 'fun' into the traditional museum, as one consultee put it. This is quite different from the independent, community basis which is more typical in the United States, although that concept appears to be gaining ground in Europe.

A related consequence is that in Europe exhibitions are more likely to be specialist and children's museums to consist of just one exhibition at a time, leading some to argue that these are not children's museums, but rather an improved museum education service. This contrasts with the multiplicity and multifunctionality of the typical US museum, but then others argue that they are not museums but activity centres for children! Furthermore, in Europe exhibitions are likely to be produced to a high, professional quality, while a US museum will be more relaxed about producing something that is more obviously home-made.

It is also apparent that European children's museums do not have the same emphasis on children visiting with their parents and on the interaction between children and adults as part of their visitor experience. It is more likely in Europe that children will visit alone or in organised parties, and that provision will be made for adults to wait somewhere apart while the children enjoy the visit.

In Europe there is a strong emphasis on the pedagogic – on the school programme planned in some detail (with the Amsterdam Kindermuseum the extreme example); while in the United States the emphasis is more on a balance between open visiting by parents and children and the educational programmes. There is, however, a common emphasis on children's museums being some form of link for children to the 'real' museum world.

Partly these differences will be a consequence of history but also of the available resources. An independent children's museum can do whatever it can raise funds for. A section of an existing museum is bound to reflect and serve, at least to some extent, the purpose of the host museum. Many of the European children's museums are hard-pressed for resources, space and staff in particular, and this acts as a severe restraint on any ambitions to do more and in a more varied manner.

Running a successful children's museum is labour-intensive, especially if there are to be adequate staff to work with the young visitors, explaining and doing. 'The Flying Suitcase' required at least 10 people 'on the floor' at any one time, a huge cost and one reason why such an exhibition can only realistically run for six weeks. The European model seems to favour labour-intensive work with small groups of children, using actors, singers and dancers (the Kindermuseum in Amsterdam insists on hiring professionals, others use a cheaper combination of students, job creation staff and volunteers). Museums linked to councils or to host museums in Berlin make no charge – but are reconsidering the question. The independent, Labyrinth, and those in The Netherlands have a clear policy of charging, but that does not cover the full cost of operation and especially of researching and developing new exhibitions. As in the

United States, children's museums are dependent on the Lottery, on private sector sponsorship and on applications to foundations. In Europe greater support from the public sector can still be expected, but for how much longer?

The relationship with schools and teachers is interestingly varied, ranging from the closely co-operative to the distinctly uneasy and suspicious. Some museums expect schools to do a considerable amount of preparation before a visit and encourage project and follow-up work afterwards. By contrast, one dismisses the teachers for the three hours of the visit so that they do not interfere with or inhibit the experience offered by the museum staff. In another, teachers are permitted to remain but only because they are responsible for their charges and therefore for discipline.

Social context and contemporary social issues form an important framework and guiding motivation for European children's museums: the increase of multicultural societies, tensions between immigrant and indigenous populations, coming to terms with history, the abrupt political, social and economic changes in eastern Europe, gay and lesbian life, children's rights. The socio-political awareness seems to be sharper in Europe than in the United States, a view apparently confirmed by a United States visitor to Europe writing in 1996:

> '"Happenings", community activism, even street theater seem to be equally legitimate sources from which to draw inspiration ... Even though I heard stories about exhibits that stirred controversy, there seemed to be a greater awareness of ideology: political, social and/or spiritual, as a necessary factor in generating programs and exhibits.'[15]

The European children's museums have been quick to develop exchanges of exhibits. It is accepted practice that specific exhibitions or exhibits designed by and used in one museum will be sold or rented (and sometimes loaned) to other museums (for example the existing collaboration between Neues Universum and Zoom Kindermuseum in Vienna; the joint venture between KJM Prenzlauer Berg and Munich). This expanding market, which can only increase as the European Network strengthens, makes it easier for a new museum initiative to start, knowing that its first main exhibition has been a proven success elsewhere (in the way Labyrinth is using Bubbles from Vienna). The children's museum in Brussels now not only has four exhibits for sale or hire but has prepared draft model agreements. Collaboration and co-operation will thus be a powerful factor in helping the children's museum movement in Europe to grow.[16]

hard or soft?

CHAPTER FIVE

When is a museum
noT a museum?

photo: Ming de Nasty

Alice sighed wearily. 'I think you might do something better with the time,' she said, 'than wasting it in asking riddles that have no answers.'[1]

The answer to our riddle is that 'museum' is probably the wrong word – perhaps especially in Britain because of its various associations – for the institutions known as children's museums which have developed in their own special way and evolved into multifunctional resource centres for children and families. It is, however, less important to debate the relevance of the word or phrase than to be clear just what a children's museum is, or might be, and what it does. Ultimately the phrase can attain a meaning of its own, as has begun to happen in the United States, such that people understand a 'children's museum' for what it is and what it does without further reference to other connotations of the word 'museum'.

It is important to emphasise that 'children's museums' are quite special and different from 'museums', yet they are hard to define and to describe to people who have not visited them and experienced them. It truly is a case of needing to see in order to believe and it is generally those who have visited the United States who become enthusiasts. Wilhelm Schmidt, a German parliamentarian, describes, not untypically, how: 'my family and I were "turned on" to the concept of children's museums and I imagined something like this in Germany' such that he 'recommended to my fellow parliamentarians … that we need to actively demand to begin working on a children's museum'.[2]

An additional dilemma in defining and describing the children's museum is that each one is different: 'Ultimately we want to create something unique, something unparalleled; we don't want to adopt, one-to-one, a museum model meant for another cultural audience, another community.'[3] This sense of individualism, related to the local community, becomes one of the great strengths of children's museums.

Taking the United States and the European experience together it is possible to discern four 'tendencies' within which children's museums have their roots, some in more than one, depending on the starting point of their initiators.

- The educational tendency: the aim to supplement the educational facilities and services available to children and their parents.

- The museological tendency: to create a museum for children which will entice children into using museums and with a strong curatorial dimension.

- The child development tendency: to provide opportunities and facilities for more stimulating learning by children and to support parents (and carers) in their roles.

- The community development tendency: where the children's museum is seen as part of wider community programmes and is likely to address social issues.

It is the overlap between these tendencies and the interaction between them that lie at the heart of the children's museum dynamic – which makes the phenomenon undefinable but unique, captivating if capricious.

Key characteristics

Most children's museums will recognise the four key characteristics which were identified in Chapter one:

- serving the needs of children, for the most part up to 12 years;

- although child-focused, equally an institution for the family, offering opportunities for children and adults to learn and play together;

- aiming to encourage learning – about society, about life, about the environment, about different cultures, about past, present and future, about anything that is considered appropriate – through discovery, through play, through fun, through experience and through exploration;

- rooted in its local community, reflecting local customs, characteristics and needs.

To this list might be added a fifth potential characteristic, namely to seek to involve children and young people in devising and planning the work of the museum and, increasingly, in its governance.

The recognition of these characteristics binds together what would otherwise be a singularly diverse range of institutions. Although there will be some from the museological tendency in Europe who will dismiss US children's museums as 'activity superstores', and others who will dismiss museums with a single exhibit directed at children as no more than good museum education, in general the movement (for such it is) shows great tolerance of diversity and a consuming interest in what others are trying to do, and how they are doing it. Thus Aaron Goldblatt on the Amsterdam Kindermuseum:

> 'I confess that my first reaction was less than enthusiastic. From my background with child-directed and visitor-controlled experiences, this programme strategy

struck me as bordering on tyrannical, the degree of control felt heavy-handed. On the second day of my visit, however, when I had a chance to watch a school group engage with the exhibit, I saw the wisdom of the approach and how well it works.'[4]

Children and governance

Meticulous care is taken, when devising and developing new exhibits for a children's museum, to ensure that they will engage the target audience and enable them to learn as well as have fun. Exhibits are tested and modified in the light of children's reactions and views. There are opportunities for comments and suggestions. As child-centred organisations the museums concentrate their resources on ensuring that they serve the needs of children.

Older children and young people are frequently involved as volunteers, thus retaining a strong link with the museum which they may have frequented as 'customers' when younger. As volunteer staff they will be likely to have some input into planning and shaping the activities of the museum.

Customer or consumer research when developing exhibits and programmes, and volunteer involvement are, however, not the same as having a place as of right in the governance or advisory structures of the organisations. At the same time, given the target age-range of children's museums, it is difficult to see how involvement structures might be devised which will be more than tokenistic (such as for example, a representative on the board or a relatively powerless youth advisory group) and which can give children and young people serious input into the governance and the behaviour of the institution. It has to be recognised that, ultimately, it is adults who create these institutions and are legally responsible for what they do and how they do it.

The 'stakeholder consultation' concept developed by the present author and the New Economics Foundation in its social audit work might be appropriate.[5] This recognises that organisations have many stakeholder groups: that is, groups who are affected by (or who can affect) the organisation. All stakeholder groups should have the right to be consulted about how they view the performance of the organisation in respect of its objectives; and in that way they may contribute to the ongoing process of monitoring and evaluation and to changes in practice and behaviour and, indeed, to the relevance of the stated objectives. Consultation of the different stakeholders must be regular and systematic, and must include all the key groups. Furthermore there is a recognition that all views require to be synthesised and that different groups may

photo: Gary Kirkham

The 'Start' interactive art exhibition at the Walsall
Museum and Art Gallery brought paintings to life for
younger children through sound, touch and smell.

well have different priorities and different perceptions. The concept also recognises that the consultation process for each stakeholder group must be devised appropriately, making it possible for the group to contribute its perceptions freely and frankly. In this way the target age-groups of a children's museum could acquire both the right to influence and the means of influencing the organisation and the governance of the institution.

European opportunities

In her presentation to the 1993 conference in Berlin, Gail Dexter Lord identified six trends which suggest that children's museums might become more common in Europe in the next years.[6]

- The demographic factor: Europe is experiencing a 'baby boom echo' from the early 'baby boomers' of the 1960s.

- Parents are better educated and therefore more likely to seek cultural and educational activities for their children.

- Children's museums meet two important, and very real, needs: they are places where families can have fun, making the most of the decreasing leisure time that many people have, and they are places offering information and support to parents.

- Children's museums are cost-effective institutions, achieving higher levels of attendance and income per square foot than other types of museums.

- Children's museums have been successful in adapting disused and derelict buildings to their needs, often as part of an inner-city revitalisation.

- An increasing awareness of the rights of children, together with the demand that cultural institutions be more accessible to people from all social and economic backgrounds, favour children's museums which explore social and cultural issues and respond positively to the concept of children's rights.

This last point is especially European rather than US. In Europe growing attention is being paid to ensuring that the rights of children are respected and upheld in law and to seeking effective ways in which children might play a part in the governance of the institutions which affect them and contribute meaningfully to community affairs. Wolfgang Zacharias writes:

'Childhood is a proper status and not just a preliminary stage into adulthood. This status needs an infrastructure similar to the wide range of adult cultural activities ... The children's museum can be seen as part of the children's rights discussion. Children have an active role in the development of the museum. They are not just visitors, they are curators, the representatives, the creators.'[7]

By contrast the United States is one of only six members of the United Nations not to have endorsed the Convention on the Rights of the Child. Thus it is curiously one of the few remaining parts of the world where there is no formal obligation to take account of children's views.

Contrasts

In Europe, as we have seen, many of those organisations which identify themselves as children's museums are in fact a section or a gallery of another, more traditional, institution which has been developed especially for a target audience of children. No matter how hands-on and exciting these may be, they are unlikely to have the same community roots which have been observed in the United States, nor to play the same multifunctional role in the community and in regard to child development and parenting services.

Similarly in Britain, those institutions (apart from Eureka!) which come closest to the children's museum idea, the science discovery centres, do not by their very nature have the breadth of focus which one would expect from a children's museum. One of the key, dynamic features of the children's museum is the way in which it combines science, culture, history, geography, human relations and all other aspects which make up the context in which children live and learn.

A further difference between European and US practice may be the desire in Europe for exhibits to be more 'professional' and 'sophisticated' whereas in the United States there is a more relaxed acceptance of what in the west of Scotland would be termed 'hand-knitted' – that is exhibits devised locally and built from whatever comes to hand. Henk Jan Gortzak puts it very plainly:

'When I first visited (the Exploratorium) 17 years ago I thought it was awful. The exhibits are eyesores ... but these exhibitions were made by employees who, in fact, actually worked with children, who, in fact, actually experimented with science. That is of real value and explains the enthusiasm of the visitors.'[8]

The children's museums in Europe visited as part of this study laid a very strong emphasis on dealing with contemporary social and cultural issues, even where these may be of a sensitive nature. Perhaps more than their US counterparts, they perceive their role as helping children and young people come to terms with the fast-changing society in which they will grow up. Their thrust is more sociological than either museological or pedagogic, even when located within an existing 'traditional' museum.

It has been suggested that one of the reasons why children's museums have developed in their present format more extensively in the United States than in Britain and Europe is because the state schooling system there is more rigid in its methods and uses less imaginative and exploratory techniques for learning. Thus the children's museum movement is an attempt to supply what ideally should be on offer through the schooling system.

Even if the proposition about the differences in schooling systems is correct – and it is outside the scope and competence of the present writer to judge – a compelling and valid case can be made for the encouragement and development of children's museums in Britain. They bring together the differing child-focused activities of playgroup, nursery school, after-school club, playschemes and adventure playgrounds and fuse them with the tradition of the museum, of the gallery and of the laboratory. This creates something very special which, combined with the European sociological dimension, is, and will continue to be, hard to define and describe in few words. We must settle for the fact that children's museums are quite distinct from other institutions; and each is unique, but all have common elements which resonate strongly in those who visit them and use them.

Social enterprise

Because the phrase 'children's museum' has no real significance in Britain as yet, people in this country are largely unaware of the range of activities and programmes they may engage in and the potential role they may play in communities. Nevertheless, the form – that of a social enterprise – is well known here and there are many organisations with a strong social purpose, structured similarly to the US children's museums and sustaining themselves partly from earned income, partly from grants and partly from fund-raising.

In Chapter three we saw that much of the work of children's museums does go on already in Britain through a variety of existing organisations. Were an association of children's museums to be set up in Britain, many organisations might sign up as members, although very few, if any, would demonstrate that multifunctionality described earlier. And there would be other organisations close to the children's museum concept who would not (yet) identify themselves as such.

A useful task which could be undertaken in Britain would be to build up and communicate a greater knowledge of children's museums, both to stimulate discussion about their potential in our society and, probably most important, to develop a greater capacity to network both within Britain and between Europe, the United States and elsewhere in the world.

Development models

Eureka! has been extremely successful and is likely to continue to be so. It is not, however, the best role model for future initiatives as it is not often that the very special set of circumstances that brought Eureka! to Halifax come about. Nevertheless a number of other development approaches might be tried, for example:

- The most usual in the United States has been the community development route, starting with a group of parents and teachers brought together by a dynamic individual; or starting with an action group which emerges from a local organisation, perhaps the parish or community council, a community association or a professional body (such as the Junior League in the United States).

- Within most local communities there are existing local organisations involved in children's issues who could be the focus for the development of a children's museum or discovery centre: a pre-school playgroup, the PTA of a nursery or of a primary school, a children's safety project committee or an after-school association.

- There are in Britain many social enterprise organisations which could decide to develop a children's museum or discovery centre either as a progression from what they already do (city farms, adventure playgrounds) or as a completely new initiative (local development trusts, community businesses).

- A further development option could be through the public/private/community partnerships which are often the vehicle chosen for regeneration programmes. These may already exist, or one may be especially formed for the purpose of sponsoring a children's museum or discovery centre. The current East London initiative is a good example of this approach.

Making discoveries with the Sound Dish Interactive
at the Launch Pad, The Science Museum, London.

photo: Science and Society Picture Library

- There is always scope to 'bolt on' or evolve a children's museum or discovery centre section within an existing museum or gallery or other institution.

At all times it is important to remember that it is possible, indeed usual to start small and build up, even to start 'without walls', 'learning by doing' as Claudia Haas of the Vienna Zoom Kindermuseum emphasised at the 1996 European Network conference: ' ... and start showing temporary children's exhibitions in preliminary spaces. A large number of visitors and good media coverage would be an enormous help in convincing your community that a children's museum is worthwhile.'[9]

Promoting the concept

All five of these 'development models' are possible and are not mutually exclusive. They could be encouraged in Britain by the formation of an association or perhaps of an experimental development unit. The remit of such an association or unit would be to promote in this country the full range of ideas and actions that are encompassed in the term 'children's museum'. The tasks which would help fulfil this remit are:

- To develop a library of information (including visual materials) about children's museums and related institutions in Britain, Europe, the United States and throughout the world.

- To establish an active and practical network so that interested people and individuals in this country can easily access information, contacts and advice.

- To maintain close liaison with the Association of Youth Museums in the United States and with Hands on! the European Committee for Children's and Youth Museums; and to encourage British memberships of the latter and greater participation in its work.

- To organise a series of events which publicise the children's museum idea. These might be held at regional centres and might involve people from overseas with direct experience of setting up and running children's museums of different types and in different contexts.

- To arrange at least one study tour of the United States, with a view to making it an annual event which coincides with the Interactivity Conference of the Association of Youth Museums.

- To arrange a study tour to Europe and to ensure that a British contingent attends the biennial European Network conference.

- To build up a catalogue of interactive exhibits which are available, or could be made available, for purchase or hire in Britain.

In addition to these traditional 'clearing-house' tasks there are two other proactive roles which might be undertaken:

- To play a development role with a small number of pilot community-based children's museum initiatives, assisting them though the basic planning, experimentation and fund-raising stages; encouraging them in this process to learn by doing.

- To explore the feasibility of building up a national pool of core exhibits which could be accessible to local children's museums (and to other bodies) by lease (or in some circumstances by purchase). Establishing this pool would entail researching and obtaining examples of good exhibits from abroad (either by purchase or under some licensing agreement) and devising and developing new exhibits to be produced in Britain. The purpose of the pool would be to make it easier for local children's museums to be set up, in that they could have instant access to a range of quality exhibits while developing their own local range. Indeed, in the long term a children's museum might expect to continue sourcing as many as 50% to 60% of its exhibits from the national pool while creating the remainder locally, with a more local content.[10]

Conclusions

There can be no absolute blueprint for a children's museum beyond the key characteristics defined at the beginning of this chapter. Otherwise each group or organisation will have its own particular emphasis and idea of what makes their museum special and important to its area. Diversity is one of the strengths of the movement.

The emphasis is always on learning, on exploring, on discovery. For that reason, in developing a British model it may be appropriate to adopt the term children's discovery centre or children's discovery museum for future use.

The purpose of this report has been to describe and, I hope, to stimulate interest in finding out more. While there are in Britain many examples of child-centred initiatives and ever more interactive exhibits, there are few institutions which can be recognised as children's museums on the United States model. There could be.

To achieve that goal we need to find out more about what others are doing around the world. We need to share to a greater extent what is being done throughout this country, and be prepared to experiment.

APPENDICES

photo: Science and Society Picture Library

Appendix one

The Association of Youth Museums (AYM)

The AYM is a professional organisation based in Washington DC which seeks to 'enhance the quality, expand the capacity, and further the vision of youth museums'.[1] The AYM offers a networking and information service to its members. This includes a slide library, an annual directory of members which includes statistical information as well as contact information, a bi-monthly newsletter and a quarterly journal *Hand to Hand*. AYM has developed a Standards Document and a Start-up Resource Pack, both of which are valuable aids for those at the beginning stages of the process of planning a children's museum.

One of the key roles of the Association is to bring people together each year at its annual 'Interactivity' conference, usually preceded by a special day given over to the issues and problems of starting up a new children's museum. The conference gives the opportunity for people new to the children's museum world to meet with those who have much experience and strengthens the sense of 'movement', of diverse institutions which share certain key objectives, values and ideas which bind them together.

A hundred and forty of the estimated 200 children's museums (1996) were members of the AYM. From a sample of 92 museums replying to their 1996 questionnaire, 36 had opened between 1990 and 1995; 81 of the 92 have opened in the past two decades (see table).[2]

Table 1: Children's museums: year of opening

1899-1925	2
1925-1950	5
1950-1975	4
1975-1980	11
1980-1984	13
1985-1989	21
1990-1995	36
Total	**92**

Table 2 shows the relative sizes of 89 children's museums listed in the AYM 1996 Directory which responded to that year's questionnaire.

Table 2: Children's museums: exhibition areas in square feet

up to 2,000	7
2,000-5,000	23
5,000-10,000	27
10,000-20,000	16
20,000-30,000	8
30,000+	8
Total	**89**

The AYM 1996 survey revealed that only one from a responding sample of 99 identified the over-12s as its target audience, while 81 specified up to 12 to 13. The remaining nine museums saw their audience as being 'all' people; children, teenagers and adults alike.

Appendix Two

The British Interactive Group (BIG)

The British Interactive Group (BIG) is an association and network for people interested in 'hands-on' interactive exhibits and displays. The membership numbered 121 at summer 1996 and included consultants in the design and installation of interactive displays and exhibits, fabricators of exhibits; museums, science centres and visitor attractions which have some element of interactive display; and interested individuals. An analysis of the 1996 *Directory of members* (which is circulated to all members) reveals some 45 institutions with hands-on displays and 15 designers and fabricators of interactive exhibits.[1]

In addition to the annual *Directory of members*, which gives space for members to advertise what they do, BIG publishes a quarterly newsletter, organises three or four activity meetings each year on subjects such as fabricating exhibits; evaluation; what teachers want from visits; training for explainers/demonstrators; health and safety; and 'open house' days, and holds an annual conference/general meeting. Each year there is a fabricators' week offering a programme of social events with the chance to collectively create prototypes of new exhibit ideas. The summer 1996 edition of the newsletter included an analysis of 53 applications made to the Millennium Commission for funding by projects with an interactive component.

In addition to a wide range of institutions, the BIG membership *Directory* lists some mobile displays. These include the Discovery Dome, a 'travelling hands-on science centre in a tent' operated by a London-based company, Science Projects Ltd, and the Magic Mathworks Travelling Circus from Wales which has travelled as far afield as the Orkneys and the South Island of New Zealand.

The European Network for Children's and Youth Museums

The European Network for Children's and Youth Museums (Hands on!) was created out of a conference held in Berlin in 1993: 'Children's and Youth Museums – Cultural Place with Great Future', organised by the Bundesverband der Jugendkunstschulen und Kulturpädagogischen Einrichtungen (BJKE) and supported by the German Ministry of Education and Science. Over 400 participants attended from 30 European and non-European countries demonstrating a depth of interest in the concept and establishing the need and the wish to keep in touch through a network. The proceedings of this conference were published in German in 1994 and in English in 1996.[1] They are a valuable source of information and ideas.

The Network publishes an annual newsletter, *CM Contact*, which includes a series of articles, brief information from member museums and a list of all members of the Network. The 1996 Network contact list contains 156 addresses from 22 European countries. By far the majority are German (85) with 10 each in Austria and Russia and 19 from Britain.

Subsequent European Network conferences have been held in Fulda, Germany, in 1994 and Amsterdam in 1996. Excursions were organised to children's museums in Paris in 1994 and to the United States in 1995 to take part in the AYM Interactivity conference and to visit children's museums in Philadelphia and Chicago. The next European conference will be held in Lisbon, Portugal, in October 1998.

The Network continues to build up its database, which was published in diskette form with the 1996 conference report[2] and aims to facilitate the exchange of exhibitions, programmes, designs and museum advisers throughout Europe. Its object is not only to carry on the debate about the theory of children's and youth museums but also to be practical and 'acquire common know-how in planning and direction'.[3]

Appendix four

Resource directory

In the United States

The Children's Museum of Acadiana
201 E Congress
Lafayette
LA 70501
Tel 00 1 318 232 8071

The Amazing Space
Mall of America
60 E Broadway West 216
Bloomington
MN 55425-5550
Tel 00 1 612 851 0000

Association of Youth Museums
1775 K Street NW
Suite 595
Washington
DC 20006
Tel 00 1 202 466 4144

Children's Museum of Atlanta
PO Box 7684
Atlanta
GA 30357
Tel 00 1 404 659 5437

Bay Area Discovery Museum
557 East Fort Baker
Sausalito
CA 94965
Tel 00 1 415 289 7268

The Children's Museum of Boston
300 Congress Street
Boston
MA 02210-1034
Tel 00 1 617 426 6500

The Brooklyn Children's Museum
145 Brooklyn Avenue
Brooklyn
NY 11213
Tel 00 1 718 735 4402

Chesapeake Children's Museum
PO Box 332
Arnold
MD 21012
Tel 00 1 410 266 0677

Children's Museums: Bridges to the Future
Cleveland Children's Museum
10730 Euclid Avenue
Cleveland
OH 44106-2200
Tel 00 1 216 791 7114

Clubkid
7585 France Avenue So
Centennial Lakes Plaza
Edina
MN 55435
Tel 00 1 612 831 1055

The Discovery Museums
177 Main Street
Acton MA 01720
Tel 00 1 508 264 4201

The Children's Museum in Easton
9 Sullivan Avenue
North Easton
MA 02356
Tel 00 1 508 230 3792

Garden State Discovery Museum
16 North Springdale Road
Cherry Hill
NJ 08003
Tel 00 1 609 424 1233

Children's Museum of Indianapolis
3000 N Meridean Street
Indianapolis
IN 46208
Tel 00 1 317 924 5431

Children's Museum of Maine
PO Box 4041
142 Free Street
Portland
ME 04101
Tel 00 1 207 828 1234

Minnesota Children's Museum
10 W 7th Street
St Paul
MN 55102
Tel 00 1 612 225 6001

Pittsburgh Children's Museum
10 Children's Way
Pittsburgh
PA 15218
Tel 00 1 412 322 5059

Please Touch Museum
210 North 21st Street
Philadelphia
PA 19103
Tel 00 1 215 963 0667

The Children's Museum of Portsmouth
280 Marcy Street
Portsmouth
NH 03801
Tel 00 1 603 436 3853

The Children's Museum of Rhode Island
58 Walcott Street
Pawtucket
RI 02860-4111
Tel 00 1 401 726 2591

Children's Museum of Southeastern Connecticut
409 Main Street
Niantic
CT 06357
Tel 00 1 860 691 1255

Staten Island Children's Museum
1000 Richmond Terrace
Staten Island
NY 10301
Tel 00 1 718 273 2060

Children's Museum of Virginia
420 High Street
Portsmouth
VA 23704
Tel 00 1 804 393 8983

In Europe

Bundesverband der Jugendkunstschulen und Kulturpädagogischen Einrichtungen (BJKE)
Luisenstrasse 22
59425 Unna
Germany
Tel 00 49 2302 69324

Hands On! European Network
Museum voor Volkenkunde Rotterdam
Willemskade 25
NL-3016 Rotterdam
The Netherlands
Tel 00 31 10 411 1055

Het Kindermuseum
Tropenmuseum
Mauritzkade 63
PO Box 95001
1090 HA Amsterdam
The Netherlands
Tel 00 31 20 568 8233

Het Reispaleis
Museum voor Volkenkunde Rotterdam
Willemskade 25
NL-3016 Rotterdam
The Netherlands
Tel 00 31 10 411 1055

Jugendmuseum in Schöneberg
Hauptstrasse 40/42
10827 Berlin
Germany
Tel 00 49 30 7876 2176

Juniormuseum
Museum für Völkerkunde
Lansstrasse 8
14195 Berlin-Dahlem
Germany
Tel 00 49 30 8301 255 434

Kinder und JugendMuseum im Prenzlauer Berg
Schiverbeiner Strasse 45
10439 Berlin
Germany
Tel 00 49 30 444 7326

Labyrinth Kinder Museum
Osloer Strasse 12
13359 Berlin
Germany
Tel 00 49 30 494 53 48

Le Musée des Enfants/Het Kindermuseum
15 rue du Bougmestre
1050 Bruxelles
Belgium
Tel 00 32 2 6400 107

Neues Universum
at Xantener Strasse 7
10707 Berlin
Germany
Tel 00 49 30 883 1103

New Metropolis
Oosterdok 2
1011 VX Amsterdam
The Netherlands
Tel 00 31 20 531 32 33

Spectrum
Deutsches Technikmuseum
Trebbiner Strasse 9
D-10963 Berlin
Germany
Tel 00 49 30 254 840

Zoom Kindermuseum
Kindermuseum im Museumsquartier
Messeplatz
Vienna
A-1070
Austria
Tel 00 43 1 522 6748

In the UK

Almond Valley Heritage Trust
Millfield
Livingston Village
Livingston
West Lothian EH54 7AR
Tel 01506 414957

British Interactive Group
Membership Secretary
Satrosphere
19 Justice Mill Lane
Aberdeen AB1 2EQ
Tel 01224 213232

Buckfast Abbey
Education Department
Buckfastleigh
Devon TQ11 0EE
Tel 01364 642519

**Children's Discovery Centre:
East London**
Stratford Development Partnership Ltd
30 Romford Road
London E15 4BZ
Tel 0181 519 7790

Clued-up Kids
Community Involvement Branch
Strathclyde Police
27 Green Street
Saltcoats
Ayrshire KA21 5HQ
Tel 01294 468236

Curioxity
The Old Fire Station
40 George Street
Oxford OX1 2AQ
Tel 01865 247004

Discovery
Brewers Quay
Hope Square
Old Harbour
Weymouth
Dorset DT4 8TR
Tel 01305 789007

Discovery Dome
Science Projects Ltd
20 St James Street
London W6 9RW
Tel 0181 741 2305

The Discovery Factory
60 Hereford Road
London W2 5AJ
Tel 0171 229 0070

Drusilla's Park
Alfriston
East Sussex BN26 5QS
Tel 01323 870656

Eureka! The Museum for Children
Discovery Road
Halifax HX1 2NE
Tel 01422 330069

The Exploratory
Bristol Old Station
Temple Meads
Bristol BS1 6QU
Tel 0117 907 9000

Flambards Village Theme Park
Helston
Cornwall TR13 0GA
Tel 01326 574549

The Guide Association
17-19 Buckingham Palace Road
London SW1W 0PT
Tel 0171 834 6242

Hazard Alley
The Safety Centre
18 Carters Lane
Kiln Farm
Milton Keynes MK11 3ES
Tel 01908 263009

Jodrell Bank Science Centre and Arboretum
Macclesfield
Cheshire SK11 9DL
Tel 01477 571339

Kelvingrove Art Gallery and Museum
Glasgow G3 8AG
Tel 0141 287 2700

The Magic Mathworks Travelling Circus
The Old Coach House
Pen-y-Pylle
Brynford
Holywell
Clwyd CH8 8HB
Tel 01352 713014

Museum of East Anglian Life
Stowmarket
Suffolk IP14 1DL
Tel 01449 612229

Museum of Childhood
42 High Street
Edinburgh EH1 1TG
Tel 0131 529 4142

Museum of Childhood
Cambridge Heath Road
London E2 9PA
Tel 0181 983 5200

Museum of the Moving Image
South Bank
Waterloo
London SE1 8XT
Tel 0171 928 3535

Natural History Museum
Cromwell Road
London SW7 5BD
Tel 0171 938 9123

Satrosphere
19 Justice Mill Lane
Aberdeen AB1 2EQ
Tel 01224 213232

Science Museum
Exhibition Road
London SW7 2DD
Tel 0171 938 8080

SEARCH
50 Clarence Road
Gosport
Hampshire PO12 1BU
Tel 01705 501957

Techniquest
Stuart Street
Cardiff CF1 6BW
Tel 01222 475 475

Ulster Museum
Botanic Gardens
Belfast BT9 5AB
Tel 01232 383000

Walsall Museum and Art Gallery
Lichfield Street
Walsall WS1 1TR
Tel 01922 653116

Windmill Hill City Farm
Phillip Street
Bedminster
Bristol BS3 4DU
Tel 0117 963 3252

Appendix Five

Museums and other institutions visited

In the United States

The Amazing Space, the Mall of America, Minnesota
The Children's Museum of Boston
The Children's Museum in Easton, MA
The Children's Museum of Maine
The Children's Museum of Portsmouth, NH
The Children's Museum of Rhode Island
The Children's Museum of South Eastern Connecticut
The Discovery Museums, Acton, MA
The Minnesota Children's Museum
The Salem Witches Museum
The Science Museum of Boston
The Science Museum of Minnesota

In Britain

The Almond Valley Heritage Centre, West Lothian
Eureka!, Halifax
The Exploratory, Bristol
Eyemouth Community Museum
Flambards Village Theme Park, Cornwall
Glenmore Heritage Centre, Ardnamurchan

Hazard Alley, Milton Keynes
Kelvingrove Art Museum and Gallery, Glasgow
Museum of Childhood, Edinburgh
Museum of Childhood, London
Museum of East Anglian Life, Stowmarket
Museum of the Moving Image, London
The Natural History Museum, London
The Royal Cornwall Museum, Truro
The Royal Museum of Scotland, Edinburgh
Satrosphere, Aberdeen
The Science Museum, London
Techniquest, Cardiff
Windmill Hill City Farm, Bristol

In Europe

Jugendmuseum, Schöneberg, Berlin
Junior Museum, Dahlem, Berlin
Kindermuseum, Amsterdam
Kinder und JugendMuseum im Prenzlauer Berg, Berlin
Labyrinth Kindermuseum, Wedding, Berlin
New Metropolis, Amsterdam
Het Reispaleis, Rotterdam
Spectrum, Berlin

Persons consulted

In the United States

Elaine Brown, the Children's Museum of Boston

Deborah Gilpin, the Discovery Museums, Acton

Bill Greaves, Greaves, Finch & Associates

Anni Gunderson, The Amazing Space

Elaine Heumann Gurian, Consultant

Nancy Kolb, Please Touch Museum, Philadelphia

Tony Mollica, Children's Museum of South Eastern Connecticut

Janice O'Donnell, Children's Museum of Rhode Island

Paula Peterson, Children's Museum in Easton

Marilyn Solvay, the Children's Museum of Maine

And scores of people who so willingly shared their ideas and experiences with me during Interactivity '96

In Britain

David Collett, Consultant

Paul Curno, Calouste Gulbenkian Foundation

Elaine Dunsire, Almond Valley Heritage Centre

Bruce Drurie, Director, Eureka!

Linda Echlin, Clued-up Kids, Ayrshire

Siân Ede, Calouste Gulbenkian Foundation

Stephen Feber, Chief Executive, World of Glass, St. Helens

Fiona Glass, The Discovery Factory

Edwin Goodall, Satrosphere

Miriam Harris, Consultant, previously of the Vivien Duffield Foundation

Colin Johnson, Techniquest

Brenda King, Hazard Alley

Gerison Lansdown, Children's Rights Office

Crawford Laughlan, Eureka!

Melian Mansfield, Campaign for State Education

Hazel Moffatt, Consultant, former HMI of Schools

Mike Primarolo, Windmill Hill City Farm

Bill Rooth, Piece Hall Traders' Association

Sara Selwood, Policy Studies Institute

Paul Sheehan, Deputy Chief Executive, Calderdale Borough Council

Richard Steckel, Consultant, and former Director, the Children's Museum of Denver

Gillian Thomas, Chief Executive, Bristol 2000

Iain Tuckett, Coin Street Community Builders

In Europe

Susanne Lembke, Labyrinth Berlin

Marie Lorbeer, Kinder und JugendMuseum im Prenzlauer Berg

Sannette Naeye, Kindermuseum Amsterdam

Helga Schmidt-Thomsen, Neues Universum Berlin

Ina Tautorat, Juniormuseum Berlin

Fred Wartna, Het Reispaleis Rotterdam and European Network

Petra Zwarcke, Jugendmuseum Schöneberg

References

Introduction

1 *A commitment to children – hope for the future*, unpublished manifesto statement of the Calouste Gulbenkian Foundation, London, 1995.

Chapter one

1 *Some facts about who we are and what we do* (The Children's Museum of Boston).

2 Sara Selwood, *Cabinets of Curiosity* (Arts Council with Calouste Gulbenkian Foundation, 1994).

3 Jane Jerry, 'What's in a name?' in *Hand to Hand* (Association of Youth Museums (AYM), vol. 5, no. 4, 1991).

4 Ann W Lewin, 'Playing to learn', in *Hand to Hand* (AYM, vol. 5, no. 4, 1991).

5 Christopher Dolgos, 'Heads up! Hands on!' in *Internation* (Rochester Children's Museum, 1996).

Chapter two

1 This quotation of Albert Einstein is to be found as a motto in many children's museums and their publications.

2 A A Milne, *The House at Pooh Corner* (Methuen, 1928).

3 K McDougall, 'Building on the tried and true', presentation to the Start-up Pre-conference, Association of Youth Museums (AYM), 1996.

4 *The Discovery Museums Exhibit Plan* (The Discovery Museums, Acton, March 1996). I am most grateful to The Discovery Museums for permission to reproduce their material.

5 K McDougall, *op cit.*

6 Patricia Steuert and others, *Opening the Museum: History and Strategies toward a more Inclusive Institution* (The Children's Museum of Boston, 1993).

7 *Museum Profile* (The Children's Museum of Boston).

8 *Ibid.*

9 Mindy Duiz, 'Commitment to community: the museum as a good citizen', in Nel Worm (ed.) *Hands On! Children's and Youth Museums: Cultural Place with Great Future* (BJKE-LKD Verlag, 1996).

10 *Ibid.*

11 Bonnie Pitman, discussion paper at Interactivity Conference, Bay Area Discovery Museum, 1996.

12 *Museum Profile* (The Children's Museum of Boston).

13 Information sheets (The Discovery Museums, April 1996) (see also The Discovery Museums *Annual Report 1994*).

14 *Ibid.*

15 *Museum Profile* (The Children's Museum of Boston).

16 *What do we do NOW?* information leaflet of The Children's Museum of Atlanta.

17 Patricia Steuert and others, *op cit.*

18 *Volunteering*, leaflet of The Children's Museum of South Eastern Connecticut (CM of SE Connecticut) and *Building Blocks*, vol. 4, issue 2 (CM of SE Connecticut).

19 *Museum Profile* (The Children's Museum of Boston).

20 Patricia Steuert and others, *op cit.*

21 *Ibid.*

22 Sue Klasky, 'Kids (big and little) discover Acton Museums', article in *Beacon Community Newspapers*, 16 November 1995.

23 'Elbow grease and dedication', article in *Down East Magazine* (The New Children's Museum of Maine, 1993).

24 *1996 Membership Directory* (AYM, Washington).

25 *Ibid.*

26 Lou Casagrande, 'Envisioning the children's museum of tomorrow', in *What's News* (The Children's Museum of Boston, 1994).

27 Robin Simons and others, *Non-profit piggy went to market: how the Denver children's museum earns $600,000 annually* (The Children's Museum of Denver, 1994).

28 Publicity leaflet of The Amazing Space, Mall of America, Minnesota.

Chapter three

1 John and Elizabeth Newsom, Foreword to the *Business Plan* of the Children's Experience Centre Ltd (CEC), 1983.

2 Ancient Chinese proverb quoted from Kate Torkington, 'The Rationale for experiential/participatory learning', Working Paper 16 in *Early Childhood Development* (Bernard van Leer Foundation, 1996).

3 *Business Plan* of the CEC, 1983.

4 *Ibid.*

5 Background information published by Eureka! The Museum for Children, 1996.

6 *Ibid.*

7 *Ibid* (see also *The Souvenir Museum Guide*).

8 *Business Plan* of the CEC, 1983.

9 The Maritime Museum in Exeter has since closed down.

10 *Directory* (British Interactive Group (BIG), 1996).

11 *Ibid.*

12 *... just like drawing in your dinner ...* (Walsall Museum and Art Gallery, 1996).

13 Dr Sally Montgomery, 'Science coaching', in *Museums Journal*, November 1993.

14 *Guide* to the Science Museum, 1996.

15 Satrosphere information sheets, 1996.

16 Quoted in *The Exploratory's Adventures in Science* (The Exploratory, 1995).

17 *The Exploratory's Adventures in Science* (The Exploratory, 1995).

18 *Ibid.*

19 Information pack, Techniquest, 1996 (see also *Techniquest in Cardiff Bay – the first ten years*).

20 *Curioxity: a review* (The Oxford Trust, 1991).

21 Publicity leaflet for Discovery, 1996.

22 *Directory* (British Interactive Group (BIG) 1996).

23 Publicity leaflet for Almond Valley Heritage Trust's Livingston Mill, 1996.

24 *Clued-up Kids: Options for Development*, Community Enterprise Consultancy and Research, report for the Safe Three Towns Project, 1996 (unpublished).

25 Because of reductions in public sector expenditure the Safe Three Towns Project closed in 1997, which was therefore the last year of Clued-up Kids.

26 Hazard Alley Safety Centre, Milton Keynes Annual Report and Accounts 1995 (see also *Clued-up Kids: Options for Development*, Community Enterprise Consultancy and Research, report for the Safe Three Towns Project, 1996 (unpublished)).

27 Information sheet of The Discovery Factory, London, 1993.

28 Outline application to the Millennium Commission; Stratford Development Partnership Ltd for Site C: Children's Interactive Resource Centre (now Children's Discovery Centre: East London).

29 *Ibid.*

Chapter four

1 A E Lamorisse, *Le Ballon Rouge* (Methuen, 1959).

2 A A Milne, *Winnie the Pooh* (Methuen, 1926).

3 Hena Bajpal, 'The need to open more ethnic museums with special emphasis on youth and children', *Conference Book of Reference; Hands on! Cultural Diversity* (European Network of Children's and Youth Museums, 1996).

4 Nina Lim Yuson, 'The Museo Pambata', *Conference Book of Reference; Hands on! Cultural Diversity* (European Network of Children's and Youth Museums, 1996).

5 Esther van Zutphen, 'Conclusions' from *Database 1996* (Kindermuseum Amsterdam with the European Network).

6 Sannette Naeye, Background information to the exhibition 'Stories to know where to go' (Kindermuseum, Amsterdam, 1995).

7 *Ibid.*

8 *Ibid.*

9 Fred Wartna, 'Enchanted Worlds', *Conference Book of Reference; Hands on! Cultural Diversity* (European Network of Children's and Youth Museums, 1996).

10 *Ibid.*

11 *Die Jüdische Schule in der Rykestrasse: ein Museumkoffer,* leaflet of the Kinder und JugendMuseum im Prenzlauer Berg.

12 Karen Hoffman, 'Barrel-organs from Prenzlauer Berg', *Conference Book of Reference; Hands on! Cultural Diversity* (European Network of Children's and Youth Museums, 1996).

13 Marie Lorbeer, 'Kinder und JugendMuseum im Prenzlauer Berg', *Conference Book of Reference; Hands on! Cultural Diversity* (European Network of Children's and Youth Museums, 1996).

14 *Der Fliegende Koffer: zum Geleit,* Ursula Pasterk (Neues Universum and Zoom Kindermuseum, 1996).

15 Aaron Goldblatt, 'The European mix', in *Hand to Hand,* Association of Youth Museums (AYM), vol. 10, no. 1, spring 1996, reproduced in *Conference Book of Reference; Hands on! Cultural Diversity* (European Network of Children's and Youth Museums, 1996).

16 Kathleen Lippens, 'Travelling exhibitions', in *Conference Book of Reference; Hands on! Cultural Diversity* (European Network of Children's and Youth Museums, 1996).

Chapter five

1 Lewis Carroll, *Alice's Adventures in Wonderland,* 1865.

2 Wilhelm Schmidt 'Children's Museums: a case for politicising children?' in Nel Worm (ed.) *Hands on! Children's and Youth Museums: Cultural Place with Great Future* (BJKE-LKD Verlag, 1996).

3 Claudia Haas, 'Labyrinthian events in Vienna', in Nel Worm (ed.) *Hands on! Children's and Youth Museums: Cultural Place with Great Future* (BJKE-LKD Verlag, 1996).

4 Aaron Goldblatt, 'The European mix', in *Hand to Hand,* Association of Youth Museums (AYM), vol. 10, no. 1, spring 1996, reproduced in *Conference Book of Reference; Hands on! Cultural Diversity* (European Network of Children's and Youth Museums, 1996).

5 See J Pearce, P Raynard and S Zadek, *Social Audit Workbook for Small Organisations* (New Economics Foundation (NEF), 1996) and J Pearce, *Measuring Social Wealth* (NEF, 1996).

6 Gail Dexter Lord, 'Children's Museums: cultural places with a great Future' in Nel Worm (ed.) *Hands on! Children's and Youth Museums: Cultural Place with Great Future* (BJKE-LKD Verlag, 1996).

7 Wolfgang Zacharias, 'The children's museum initiative: the new cultural centre in the spirit of our time?' in Nel Worm (ed.) *Hands on! Children's and Youth Museums: Cultural Place with Great Future* (BJKE-LKD Verlag, 1996).

8 Henk Jan Gortzak, 'Non-Western cultures in Western museums' in Nel Worm (ed.) *Hands on! Children's and Youth Museums: Cultural Place with Great Future* (BJKE-LKD Verlag, 1996).

9 Claudia Haas, 'The difficulties of setting up a children's museum', *Conference Book of Reference; Hands on! Cultural Diversity* (European Network of Children's and Youth Museums, 1996).

10 I am indebted for this idea to Stephen Feber, formerly of The Children's Experience Centre and now of World of Glass, St. Helens.

Appendix one

1 *1996 Membership Directory* (Association of Youth Museums (AYM), Washington).

2 The data for Tables 1 and 2 and other facts and figures are taken from the *1996 Membership Directory* of the AYM, and from other survey information provided by the AYM.

Appendix two

1 *Directory* (British Interactive Group (BIG) 1996).

2 *Ibid.*

Appendix three

1 Nel Worm (ed.) *Hands on! Children's and Youth Museums: Cultural Place with Great Future* (BJKE-LKD Verlag, 1996).

2 *Conference Book of Reference; Hands on! Cultural Diversity* (European Network of Children's and Youth Museums, 1996) and *Database 1996* (Kindermuseum Amsterdam with the European Network).

3 Claudia Haas in Nel Worm (ed.) *Hands on! Children's and Youth Museums: Cultural Place with Great Future* (BJKE-LKD Verlag, 1996).